So You Want to be a Dean?

Pathways to the Deanship

Edited by

Kate Conley
William & Mary

and

Shaily Menon
University of New Haven

Series in Education
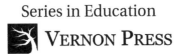 VERNON PRESS

In the Americas:
Vernon Press
1000 N West Street, Suite 1200,
Wilmington, Delaware 19801
United States

In the rest of the world:
Vernon Press
C/Sancti Espiritu 17,
Malaga, 29006
Spain

Series in Education

Library of Congress Control Number: 2022934832

ISBN: 978-1-64889-195-3

Cover design by Vernon Press.

Table of Contents

Acronyms

AAC&U	American Association of Colleges and Universities
A&S	Arts and Sciences
ACE	American Council on Education
ADVANCE	NSF programs for Organizational Change for Gender Equity in STEM
Alt-Ac	Alternate Academic
APAHE	Asian Pacific Americans in Higher Education
BIPOC	Black, Indigenous People of Color
CAL	College of Arts and Letters at Northern Arizona University
CC	Colorado College
CCAS	Council of Colleges of Arts and Sciences
CDC	Center for Disease Control and Prevention
CDO	Chief Diversity Officer
CEO	Chief Executive Officer
CLAS	College of Liberal Arts and Sciences, Grand Valley State University
CMU	Central Michigan University
COLL	College Curriculum at William & Mary
COVID-19	Coronavirus disease 2019
CSWP	Committee on the Status of Women in the Profession
CU	University of Colorado
DEI	Diversity, Equity, and Inclusion
EPC	Educational Policy Committee
FEC	Faculty Executive Committee, Colorado College
FERPA	Family Educational Rights and Privacy Act
FTE	Full-time equivalent
GE	General Education
GED	General Education Development Test
GIS	Geographic Information System
Grad Gen 1	First-generation graduate students
GSC	Graduate Student Council, Harvard University

GVSU	Grand Valley State University
H2C	Here to Career, Here 2 Career, University of Massachusetts, Amherst
HEC	Humanities Executive Committee, Colorado College
HERS	Higher Education Resource Services for Women in Higher Education Leadership
HFA	College of Humanities and Fine Arts, University of Massachusetts, Amherst
HR	Human Resources
HSS	College of Humanities and Social Sciences, CSU, Fullerton
IU	Indiana University
LEAP	Liberal Education and America's Promise
LGBTQ+	Lesbian, Gay, Bisexual, Transsexual, Queer +
LSAT	Law School Admission Test
MLA	Modern Language Association
MTSU	Middle Tennessee State University
NAU	Northern Arizona University
NSF	National Science Foundation
PhD	Doctor of Philosophy
POC	People of Color
POROI	Project on the Rhetoric of Inquiry, University of Iowa
PWI	Predominantly White Institutions
PR	Public Relations
PTA	Parent Teacher Association
R-1	Research-One universities: very high research activity
R-2	Research-Two universities: high research activity
RCM	Responsibility Centered Management
SCH	Student credit hours
SFSU	San Francisco State University
SLACs	Selective small liberal arts colleges
SUNY	State University of New York
STEM	Science, Technology, Engineering, and Math
TA	Teaching Assistant
TEAC	Teacher Education Accreditation Council
TT	tenure-track faculty

TU	Tulsa University
UC	University of Cincinnati
UMaine	University of Maine
UMass	University of Massachusetts
USD	University of South Dakota
UVA	University of Virginia
WGS	Women's and Gender Studies

Introduction

Kate Conley

William & Mary

Shaily Menon

University of New Haven

Abstract

This volume comprises essays by humanist and interdisciplinary arts and sciences faculty who became academic deans, with reflections on how each of them used their position to further the liberal arts, fulfill special projects, and play a leadership role in shared governance on their campuses. The volume grew out of a series of panels co-sponsored by the Modern Language Association (MLA) and the Council for Colleges of Arts and Sciences (CCAS), the professional organization to which these deans belong. The essays are designed to serve as brief reflections that together provide a textured overview of what to expect in the transition to the deanship, how the responsibility of being dean can be used to benefit faculty colleagues and goals, and why the willingness to take on such a sizable administrative role matters. The essays are organized in three sections: Leadership as Journey, Leadership for Institutional Change, and Leadership Preparation. Recognizing the power of storytelling in their role as leaders, the essays share the stories of how these colleagues were motivated to join the administration in public and private, large and small institutions, how their career pathways led them there, what their jobs entailed, what were some of the satisfactions they derived from their work, and, in some cases, how they felt about the experience.

Keywords: arts and sciences, assistant dean, associate dean, college, Council of Colleges of Arts and Sciences (CCAS), COVID-19, dean, faculty, faith, feminism, institutional change, interdisciplinarity, journey, leadership, literature, Modern Language Association (MLA), narrative theory, pandemic, storytelling, university

***

This volume of essays was conceived as part of a Modern Language Association panel held in the moments before COVID-19 became a household name. In

January 2020, COVID-19 was known only to those closely following health news and, in Seattle that month, it seemed like an illness limited to a handful of cases that were being monitored outside the city limits, well beyond the Convention Center where the panel took place. The authors of these essays started their leadership journeys well before 2020 and that preparation helped them navigate their colleges and institutions through the uncertain times that followed.

Few of the authors in this collection set out to become administrators. Many of the narratives begin with personal stories of deans who started their university careers as first-generation students and then became faculty members themselves seemingly by chance, and whose rise to leadership was partly rooted in gratitude for the opportunities higher education afforded. Many of us have found the work rewarding because we can work collaboratively, give back to our institutions, be accountable to the faculty we serve, and dedicate our creativity to further the dreams we recognize in our students and colleagues.

The Council of Colleges of Arts & Sciences (CCAS) is a professional organization for deans in the arts and sciences with the mission of "Empowering Deans to Lead." As part of our outreach to arts and sciences faculty, the CCAS Board organizes panels at the annual meetings of arts and sciences deans, associate & assistant deans, and faculty in a variety of disciplines. Our purpose is to encourage faculty colleagues to realize they can and should consider and assume administrative positions. We answer faculty questions about what it is like to serve as an academic dean, what the job is like, how we got our jobs, what kinds of preparation we had, and what sorts of goals have motivated us. Informally, the Board calls these panels, "So You Want to be a Dean?" Members of the CCAS Board volunteer to chair panels at our own professional conventions. As we describe above, the essays here grew out of a panel held at the last pre-pandemic Modern Language Association meeting in Seattle, Washington, in January 2020. An editor for Vernon Press, who was in the audience, expressed interest in publishing a book of essays based on the panel. We discussed this possibility at the next CCAS Board meeting and decided to pursue the project. This volume is the result.

We recognize the power of storytelling that deans wield in their role as leaders and so we encouraged them to tell their personal stories, to focus on projects that motivated them, to reflect also on how they kept their faculty and staff motivated and, when appropriate, to review the impact of the pandemic on their most recent work. The lessons we have learned can serve as advice for those who are already serving deans and also for those who are about to become deans. We hope so.

The first section focuses on essays that tell the story of leadership as a journey: from the sciences through the arts to the arts and sciences (Menon); from an academic background in feminism to a feminist style of leadership

(Conley); from training in narrative theory to deploying narrative in order to lead (Massé); how a background in history and a grounding in faith served as preparation for coping with a pandemic (Hall); and how training in literature and culture helped provide resources and solutions for leading through change and a pandemic (Ferme). The second section comprises essays that describe leading institutional change such as heading a faculty through a process of becoming an antiracist campus (Garcia); founding a new College of Liberal Arts and Sciences (Antczak); becoming Dean at your home institution (Gunzenhauser); and becoming Dean in a new institution, supported by strengths drawn from an untraditional background (Petersen). The third section focuses on ways to prepare for deanship that include trusting one's team through a crisis such as a pandemic (Fontaine); understanding how a background as an academic prepares one for deanship (Haddad); maintaining the perspective of a faculty colleague through and in leadership (Wilburn); relying on one's academic interests and values in order to effect institutional change (Hayes); and understanding that everything counts, that all of life's experiences serve as preparation for deanship (Krebs). All the deans in this volume wound up leading faculty outside of the disciplines in which they had trained and that cross-disciplinary approach, taking into account *all* of arts and sciences in their commitment to leadership, expanded their perspectives, as they recount, and made their approach inherently interdisciplinary.

We thank all our contributors for their openness to telling their stories, both professional and personal. We thank you, our readers, for your interest in the administrative work of higher education and how it is evolving and remains relevant to the changing societal landscapes around us.

Leadership as Journey

One

Work, Pilgrimage, and Identity: An Interdisciplinary Journey in Arts and Sciences

Shaily Menon

University of New Haven

Abstract

This essay shares the story of the author's journey in the liberal arts and sciences, which she began as a young girl in India fascinated by the arts and also the sciences, and which she continued through graduate study in the United States, in US laboratories and in the rainforest. It is a story of how the foundational love of both the arts and sciences led her to join the faculty and then administration in Colleges of Arts and Sciences at public and private institutions. It is also the story of an immigrant and woman of color, of representation and inclusion, of role models and mentors. The essay includes reflections on the role of liberal education, the value of the arts and sciences, the importance of shared leadership, collaborative approaches and interdisciplinary initiatives, and key lessons learned along the way—during and outside times of crises, such as the ones we are all currently navigating.

Keywords: ACE, ADVANCE, anthropology, biodiversity informatics, Biology, Campus Philly, climate change, conservation biology, distributed leadership, early-career faculty, GIS, Global Philadelphia Association, Grand Valley State University, HERS, inclusion and equity, Interdisciplinary Research Clusters, journey, leadership, liberal education, Mural Arts, Natural Resource Management, NSF, pilgrim's path, private institutions, public institutions, Saint Joseph's University, sciences, transdisciplinary approach, San Francisco State University, STEM, University of New Haven, zoology

***

In *Crossing the Unknown Sea: Work as a Pilgrimage of Identity,* the poet David Whyte describes the central concerns of leadership as similar to those of a purposeful life: taking real steps on the pilgrim's path, making everything more personal, understanding "life or leadership not as an abstract path involving devious strategies but more like an inhabitation, a way of life, a conversation, a captaincy; an expression of individual nature and gifts and a familiarity with the specific nature of your own desires and fears."[1]

This is the story of my journey in the liberal arts and sciences, which I began as a young girl in India fascinated both by the arts and the sciences and which I continued through graduate study in the United States, in US laboratories, and in the rainforest in India with the design of an interdisciplinary doctoral degree. This is the story of how the foundational love of the arts, humanities, and sciences as a child led me to become first a university faculty member and then associate dean and dean in colleges of arts and sciences at public and private institutions. This is also the story of an immigrant and woman of color, of representation and inclusion, of role models and mentors. I hope that my story will resonate with early-career faculty who are not thinking of leadership but practicing it; faculty who are facing some of the messages I did so that they can recognize the false dichotomies inherent within them.

In telling my story, I will share key moments and insights that guided and shaped my journey. Then, I will offer my reflections on the value of the arts and sciences, the role of liberal education, and the importance of collaborative and interdisciplinary approaches. Finally, I will share some lessons about shared leadership and epistemic humility I learned along the way—during and outside times of crises, such as the ones we are all currently navigating.

Messages about identity and work

The idea of "work as a pilgrimage of identity" resonates with me on many levels. Starting from a young age, we are surrounded by implicit and explicit messages about identity and work. Whether we are aware of them or not, these messages affect our choices in significant ways.

My earliest messages came from growing up in a small family of limited means, but which never suffered from a lack of library books. My interest in the sciences was sparked by books about scientists: Paul de Kruif's *Microbe Hunters* and *The Story of Madame Curie* by Alice Thorne, with illustrations by Frederico Castellon that brought the story to life. These books set my mind on fire and I was drawn to the idea of such a purposeful and adventurous life. A life of exploring language, writing, art, and the sciences.

As a young child, I became aware of implied and overt messages that girls can't or oughtn't to do science or be scientists; the public imagination was beholden to a representation of scientists as men in white lab coats. Approaching junior college, I was confronted with a choice between the arts and the sciences; it was not possible to combine the two in any significant way. The messages were that I would have to give up my interest in the arts and humanities to do science. The corollary to that message was that science is not a creative endeavor. Many of the subsequent choices I made, throughout my career, have been influenced by questioning and resisting such messages. I encountered messages that diminished the value of work done by women and minorities, confused confidence with competence in leadership, and yet others that assumed academic disciplines are immutable and threatened by interdisciplinary or transdisciplinary approaches. But more about this later.

With guidance from my parents, I enrolled in the sciences so that I had access to labs and equipment, but I also immediately signed up for a French language course at *L'Alliance Française*. It made for some long and exhausting days starting with taking the bus to French class early in the morning and ending with returning home late in the evening after chemistry lab. Yet, I was comforted by my small act of rebellion and agency against what I was convinced was a false choice. I had taught myself calligraphy and taped this aphorism above my desk throughout my school years: "Traveler, there is no path; paths are made by walking." I brought that small and, by then, sepia-toned slip of paper with me to the dorm when I came to the US for graduate school, first completing a master's thesis in circadian biology and then starting a doctoral program in anthropology.

During the first semester of my doctoral program in the late 1980s, I took required courses in linguistics, archeology, physical anthropology, and cultural anthropology, and loved them. I wanted to add courses in remote sensing of the environment, ecosystem modeling, and quantitative and theoretical ecology so I could learn the theory and practical knowledge to help me with my planned dissertation research on an endangered species in the tropical rainforest. The department denied my requests to replace some of the required anthropology courses and adding those cross-disciplinary courses would have meant an extra semester or even year of course work. In exploring the possibility of designing my own interdisciplinary doctoral program, I had to resist the fear from dire predictions by some well-meaning advisors that I would "belong nowhere academically" and would not fit in any department when it was time to look for a faculty position. I decided I would cross that bridge when I came to it. I was convinced of the value of interdisciplinary thinking, so I persisted. I was used to life at the edges, in the interstices of disciplines, which is where I felt the most exciting discoveries happened. Fortunately, other advisors supported my decision and helped me with the design of an interdisciplinary program in anthropology, zoology, and natural resources.

As I neared the completion of my doctoral degree, I presented some of my work at a Smithsonian Symposium on forest remnants in the tropical landscape. This led to an invitation to be a postdoctoral fellow tasked with establishing and leading a Conservation GIS (Geographic Information System) lab at the University of Massachusetts Boston, where I did work on biodiversity informatics, socioeconomic drivers of deforestation, and global change (land-use change, sea-level, and climate change). Those were productive years that included a difficult pregnancy due to hyperemesis. My mentor supported my time away and, subsequently, my decision to bring my daughter to work during her infancy. The presence of many researchers and visiting scientists from different countries made it an exciting and stimulating place to work. Across the hall, the Conservation Genetics lab was led by another postdoctoral fellow, originally from Sri Lanka; he has since begun his own journey into higher education administration, and I have enjoyed sharing professional development insights with him.

Three years later, in 1997, I was offered a faculty position at Grand Valley State University to help bridge the areas of Biology and Natural Resources Management that had recently been brought together in one department. My interdisciplinary doctoral degree and postdoctoral work turned out to be an asset in this task. I developed curriculum in conservation biology and spatial analysis and, in addition to teaching those courses, I taught courses in environmental ethics and systems modeling.

During my early years as a faculty member, I served as program director of Natural Resources Management and then as assistant chair of Biology. When the department chair spent a semester away, I was invited by the dean to serve as interim department chair, a risky move during the semester I was up for tenure. After much soul searching, I decided that I would do my part to serve the department; after all, it was only a semester-long obligation and I had completed the requirements for tenure and submitted my dossier. At the end of the semester, the former chair withdrew from her position, and the faculty and dean invited me to lead the department as chair. Chairing a complex department with a turbulent past, early in my tenure as a faculty member, was one of my most formative experiences. I participated in the HERS (Higher Education Resource Services) Summer Institute for department chairs at Bryn Mawr, knowing the professional development and guidance would help in the task ahead of me, and it did. As chair, I helped with strategic planning for the department and, together, we developed a set of aspirational goals. Working collaboratively, we reformed existing structures and processes, and created new ones that fully engaged faculty in the department. I oversaw the establishment of a new personnel committee; revised procedures that included formal peer evaluation of teaching rather than placing an undue emphasis on student evaluation, given well-established research on the gender and racial bias inherent in the latter.

Early in my career at Grand Valley State University, together with faculty and staff colleagues across the campus, I participated in a yearlong program called "Claiming a Liberal Education" following the model provided by AAC&U (American Association of Colleges and Universities)'s Liberal Education and America's Promise (LEAP).[2] As part of this initiative, we read key texts and research and discussed the value of liberal education, the arts and sciences, and the ongoing federal and state disinvestment, and public disenchantment with the value of higher education. This campus-wide dialog helped me find allies across campus in the other colleges, academic affairs, and student affairs. I developed a vision for the arts and sciences founded upon the idea of both/and—that is, the theoretical and the practical, applying the arts and the sciences to address real world problems. And I became even more convinced of the value of collaboration and innovation for inclusion and excellence.

All around me were messages that the work of women and that of underrepresented minorities is valued less than that of their peers. I saw that women and minority faculty were active in all levels of institutional service—much of it in the form of hidden labor—but few women and people of color achieved full professor status or served in leadership positions. This led to my participation in a collaborative project funded by the National Science Foundation (NSF), ADVANCE, which alerted me to the fact that women and people of color tend to be at a greater risk of becoming mired in service and institutional housekeeping in ways that inhibit their professional advancement. The NSF ADVANCE project was aimed at increasing the participation of women in the sciences and engineering. With colleagues in the Sciences, College of Engineering, and Women and Gender Studies at GVSU, and in collaboration with the University of Michigan, we delved into the literature on the obstacles faced by women in the academic fields of science and engineering, including gender schemas, a lack of critical mass, biased evaluations, and the accumulation of disadvantage. We focused on schemas based in stereotypes that guide social perceptions and behaviors. We learned that even small amounts of bias or very small differences of treatment can accumulate over time resulting in profound differences in salary, representation, and advancement that are more and more pronounced and measurable at higher levels of organizations or careers. A lack of critical mass also results in a lack of networking mechanisms and of mentors and role models for women. We used interactive theatre and peer mentoring to communicate concepts and data related to inclusion and equity. When the project concluded, we worked with the Division of Inclusion and Equity to formalize some of the best practices of the ADVANCE project in a university-wide Inclusion Advocate training program at GSVU.

It became clear to me that even as I advocated for and supported faculty in their professional trajectories, I was on the path to becoming a part of the problematic statistics against which I was cautioning my colleagues. After two consecutive three-year terms as department chair, and with the department in a much stronger position and much more collaborative and forward-thinking than it had been before, I made the decision to return to the faculty and work on my promotion to the rank of professor.

Not long after my promotion, I was invited by the president to chair a University Faculty Referendum Task Force, the first referendum for the university in which faculty had challenged a decision made by their elected representatives in the academic senate. Subsequently, I was invited to serve as associate dean working with the team put together by the founding dean of the College of Liberal Arts and Sciences. Each member of the dean's team received tremendous support and opportunities for leadership in their areas of responsibilities; mine were faculty research and grant support, facilities planning, strategic planning, and community engagement.

As associate dean, I had the opportunity to create a structure to bring together faculty and students from disparate disciplines. During a conversation with a colleague about the need for interdisciplinary thinking to address complex societal issues like climate change, I encountered a level of resistance that surprised me: my colleague believed that including other disciplinary approaches would be a distraction and that we needed to focus single-mindedly on the science. I was stunned by my colleague's conviction that once scientists had figured out climate change, the problem would be solved. I remember thinking, wait, what about other considerations that have contributed to the problem and could be part of the solution: ethics, values, history, culture, literature, economics, communicating messages, the psychology of resistance and denial, social justice, policymaking, political will, to name just a few?

These kinds of conversations sowed the seeds for what would become an initiative known as Interdisciplinary Research Clusters. In consultation with faculty groups across the college, we created five interdisciplinary research clusters on the themes of borders, brain, health, urban, and water. Eventually, a sixth cluster called digital was added. During its first two years, this effort generated collaborations between faculty and students from twelve disciplines and seven colleges across the university and several community partners. In 2020, four years after leaving GVSU, I was invited to give a keynote at a virtual climate change summit. I was delighted to learn that the summit was funded by a grant from the initiative I had helped to launch.

I spent 2015-16 as a fellow in the office of the president at San Francisco State University. My focus was on community engagement and design thinking for social innovation, but I also had the opportunity to obtain an insider view of crisis management, given significant social justice issues and protests during a particularly difficult year that unfolded at SFSU. As ACE (American Council for Education) Fellows, we also had the opportunity to visit several institutions across the US and meet with leaders at those institutions. These were amazing opportunities to learn about the broad spectrum of higher education institutions and the problems they face as well as their creative approaches to meeting the needs of their students.

Serving on the boards of national organizations such as the Asian Pacific Americans in Higher Education (APAHE) and the Council Colleges of Arts and Sciences (CCAS) has also provided me with a national perspective and high regard for the power of mentoring and importance of role models for professional development. I continue to benefit from my membership in these organizations and, in addition to attending their meetings, I also regularly attend the annual meetings of organizations such as ACE and the Association of American Colleges & Universities (AAC&U).

From 2017-2020, I served as dean of the College of Arts and Sciences at Saint Joseph's University and worked on developing a strategic vision and set of priorities for the college. My interdisciplinary background, in addition to my experience with program formation at GVSU, had prepared me for leading new curricular and co-curricular initiatives with an eye toward innovation and local and global engagement at Saint Joseph's. Working collaboratively with faculty, we launched new programs in art history, artificial intelligence, computational engineering, cybersecurity, data science, graphic design, Geographic Information Systems (GIS), and public policy. We created new experiential learning opportunities for students in areas such as translational medicine, cancer research, and entrepreneurship through an incubator space on campus in partnership with a local biotech startup working on a humoral immuno-oncology discovery platform and preclinical therapy. Other rewarding areas of my work at Saint Joe's included collaborating with the college advisory board on strategic initiatives, working with faculty and staff on diversity, equity and inclusion initiatives, increasing grant applications and awards in the college of arts and sciences, facilitating a partnership of the university with the renowned Barnes Foundation to promote appreciation of art and horticulture, serving on the board of Campus Philly, an organization dedicated to retaining talent in the region, and expanding arts and cultural programming through key partnerships, such as an arts and sustainability project with Global Philadelphia Association and Mural Arts.

Starting in the summer of 2021, I was invited to serve as dean of the College of Arts and Sciences at the University of New Haven and work towards advancing five strategic priorities for the university in the areas of 1) Market-Responsive Education, 2) Transformative Student Experiences, 3) Justice, Equity, Diversity, Inclusion, and Service, 4) Customized Educational Models, and 5) People First. We are exploring key partnerships in the region and working to create a university of and for the future with on-ramps for learners throughout their career. I look forward to my ongoing work with faculty and other key internal and external stakeholders as we launch innovative and interdisciplinary programs and contribute to diversity and excellence.

It is truly rewarding to have opportunities to make my own passion for cross-disciplinary problem solving accessible to students, especially in this uncertain age, which Whyte describes as "a time when much of the way we see and describe ourselves is under immense strain from the current of change that swirl around us." In the next section of this essay, I would like to explore the value of liberal education and its importance in helping students shape their future.

Claiming a Liberal Education

We live in a time when many of our most cherished institutions and values are under attack: the free press; scientific inquiry; inclusiveness and respect for people regardless of race, gender, sexual orientation, disability, or immigration status; civil discourse; the pursuit of knowledge and respect for expertise; and higher education, especially the liberal arts and sciences. It is a time that puts misplaced emphasis almost exclusively on the private good rather than on the public purposes of higher education. Following the 2008 economic collapse, which has been exacerbated by job losses due to pandemic-related shutdowns, and in the absence of a clear vocational focus, the liberal arts are deemed impractical and of little value while science is misunderstood or seen by some as a roadblock to freedom and returning to economic prosperity.

And yet, now more than ever, our world needs the skills and social values cultivated by a liberal education. Now, more than ever, our nation needs publicly engaged citizens committed to the work of social justice. Now, our community, our nation, our world needs persons prepared to think critically about the evidence before them, to distinguish truth from misinformation, persons prepared to solve problems amid the unfamiliar—agile thinkers with a broad base of knowledge from which to question, analyze, and respond more thoughtfully to an increasingly volatile, uncertain, complex, and ambiguous world.

We know that an education in the liberal arts prepares students for their first job, and more importantly, it prepares them for a lifetime of learning and for jobs that don't yet exist and haven't even yet been imagined. A liberal arts education allows us to integrate contemplation and action, so that students have well-developed and reflective minds, alongside a desire to work toward a more just and humane world. A liberal arts education helps students develop moral discernment and equips them with the tools to live out a transformative commitment to social justice. It allows us to be true to our missions and to what William Cronon, in his essay "Only Connect," describes as "exercising our freedom in such a way as to make a difference in the world and make a difference for more than just ourselves."[3] It is for these reasons that the liberal arts and sciences form the intellectual heart of education at institutions of higher education and one of the most important tasks, for us as deans of colleges of arts and sciences, is to support, secure, and sustain that centrality in the university's academic mission.

The needs of the twenty-first century and the problems we face, including climate change, unsustainable models of consumption, social injustice, and worldwide pandemics, all call for interdisciplinary approaches rooted in the arts and sciences. Amid rapid and unprecedented social, technological, and environmental change, the challenges we face will increasingly fall into the category of wicked problems rife with complex interdependencies that defy simple solutions. Solving such problems will require us to transcend disciplinary thinking and develop the ability to work collaboratively in multi-disciplinary teams without losing the integrity of disciplinary knowledge. Life-long learning and liberal education are relevant now more than ever. This affirmation bears repetition, especially in the context of political and economic turmoil and the temptation of expedient solutions. My vision for a college of arts and sciences is one in which we explore initiatives that bring together various disciplines to solve complex, real-world problems, and help faculty and students engage in collaborative and creative generation of new knowledge to benefit both their communities and their own learning. As Beth McMurtrie said in a piece in the *Chronicle of Higher Education*: "Traditional teaching may have sufficed when college campuses were more ivory tower than lifeboat, educating future generations of scholars and other elites rather than trying to lift up a diverse group of students and prepare them for an increasingly complex world."[4]

The initiatives in which I participated were open to me because I accepted the invitation to step into leadership roles. They allowed me to move beyond my personal interdisciplinary background and research focus to connect meaningfully with my university colleagues and together build community across disciplines and schools and beyond our university walls with the city where we live. In the final section of this essay, I would like to share some lessons I have learned along my journey.

Lessons for a Changing Time

The most important lessons I have learned on my journey are about values, courage, and vulnerability—the kind of leadership that David Whyte describes as "based on a courageous vulnerability that invites others by our examples to a frontier conversation whose outcome is yet in doubt." We have all experienced the devastating consequences of tolerating incompetent leaders, or worse yet, those who abandon values in a time of crisis.

The concept of distributed or shared leadership was introduced to me early in my journey during a HERS Summer Institute fireside chat presented by Beverly Daniel

Tatum, then president of Spelman College. I was relieved to know that there was a
term for the kind of leadership that naturally appealed to me. In their book on
shared leadership, Adrienne Kezar and Elizabeth Holcomb posit that higher
education requires new approaches, new forms, to meet ever growing challenges.[5]
They call for shared leadership, a model that shies away from the binary of a leader
and followers and empowers people throughout the organization to be leaders
within their spheres of influence. Elements of shared leadership are found in
organizations that have proven to be better at learning, innovating, and adapting
to the types of challenges that campuses face today. Shared leadership encourages
individuals to lead from their center and to be leaders within their spheres of
influence regardless of title. Shared leadership helped institutions in their response
to crises, such as the ongoing pandemic.

In our responses to the pandemic, we also learned the importance of epistemic
humility: being open to new knowledge and data, adapting our response as the
pandemic evolved, and being ready to admit when the response was inaccurate or
inadequate. We learned the value of clear and frequent communication, both of
institutional values as well as actions and decisions. We learned to be comfortable
with cognitive dissonance, uncertainty, and contradiction. We learned to
appreciate the wisdom in both "Look before you leap" and "One who hesitates is
lost." Deans embraced the key role they play in guiding their colleges through this
time of change and disruption. The strong teams we created, our support of faculty
and staff to be leaders in their spheres of influence, the relationships we built rooted
in humor, goodwill, and trust have carried us through crises.

We continue to be called upon to reimagine our colleges and disciplines in ways
that will meet the needs of our students so that they will have productive careers
and meaningful lives. The anxieties and uncertainties of the pandemic, social
injustice, climate change, and so many other ongoing crises, have been depleting
and exhausting for us and for our students and colleagues. We can find hope in
human ingenuity and resilience and the important role that the arts and sciences
will play to help shape our future.

And we can remind ourselves that there is no path; paths are made by walking.

Notes

[1] David Whyte, *Crossing the Unknown Sea: Work as a Pilgrimage of Identity* (New York:
Riverhead Books, 2001), 55-56.
[2] I'd like to acknowledge Catherine Frerichs (1945-2022), professor of writing and English
at Grand Valley State University and director of the pew Faculty Teaching and Learning
Center, who was one of the fearless leaders of the "Claiming a Liberal Education"
initiative and who served as a mentor and inspiration to me and many women faculty.
[3] William Cronon, "Only Connect: The Goals of a Liberal Education," *The American
Scholar* 67, no. 4 (1998): 73-80.

[4] Beth McMurtrie, "Why the Science of Teaching is Often Ignored," *The Chronicle of Higher Education*, January 3, 2022.

[5] Kezar, Adrienne and Elizabeth Holcomb, *Shared Leadership Lessons in Higher Education: Important Lessons from Research and Practice* (Washington D.C.: American Council on Education, 2017).

Two

Administration as Feminist Practice

Kate Conley

William & Mary

Abstract

This essay reflects on thirteen years as a dean and associate dean at William & Mary and Dartmouth and the opportunity administration presents to practice feminist values in higher education. Training as a humanist provided the chance to renew both universities' core commitment to the liberal arts from within the leadership of arts and sciences. Through personal example, this essay shows how administration allows for the chance to mentor junior colleagues, pay attention to previously overlooked complaints of harassment and bullying, update and systematize practices and policies, implement new action plans for diversity and inclusion, support non-tenure-track colleagues, and pursue goals such as strong and open communication within the faculty, as well as transparency and equity across arts and sciences. The benefit of being a woman in such a leadership position lies in the implicit encouragement to female students and junior faculty it offers through the visibility a woman at the helm can muster. A woman administrator can give voice to her own feminist values and make sure that the voices of her peers are heard.

Keywords: academic trajectory, accountability, arts and humanities, associate professor project, COLL curriculum, COVID-19, CSWP of the MLA, collective good, Comparative Literature, cross-disciplinary teaching, Dartmouth College, dean, diversity and inclusion, English, equity, feminism, feminist, French, global citizenship, liberal arts, literature, humanities, mentor, promotion, rank, research, scholarship, service, shared governance, surrealism, teamwork, tenure, William & Mary

***

During my thirteen years as an academic dean, I appreciated how my training as a professor of French and Comparative Literature allowed me to bring my values as a humanist to university administration, first as associate dean for the arts and humanities at Dartmouth College and then as dean of the faculty of arts and sciences at William & Mary. My scholarly background in feminist approaches to literature and culture primed me to argue for the necessity of assuring that education be as inclusive as possible—from the perspective of the curriculum and in the composition of the faculty and students. My background as an English major with a PhD in French also helped me argue for the importance of the humanities to a liberal arts education and the formation of citizens in a global society. Choosing administration constitutes a shift in an academic trajectory as a scholar-teacher, often a choice that arises as a surprise, seemingly by chance, according to the kind of "fortuitous encounter" that is deeply rooted in surrealist thought, to which I have dedicated most of my research over the past thirty years. Such a shift provides the chance to pivot from nurturing students to nurturing one's peers, to furthering the academic trajectories of others. It constitutes "service" at the most fundamental level.

This is at once my personal story—the narrative of how one faculty member came into administration, what she found the job to be like, and what she was able to do in a leadership position—and the story of my effort to bring the values I had learned through my scholarship to my work as an administrator. It's also a way for me to take stock of my years in administration as I step into one more transition—from the deanship into the classroom two years ago, and now into my final leave before retirement. As an assistant professor, I used to think of my work as oddly divided between solitary research and public performance. The last thing I thought I wanted to do was spend time in administration, partly because it seemed to be all about performance at the expense of the quiet work of research. I had been promoted without tenure in 1998, after a senior male colleague argued successfully that I worked on "minor figures in a minor movement" in my first book on women in surrealism. By the time I got tenure two years later, I didn't yet understand that in an administrative position, I might be able to do something about senior colleagues who bully and support those, like me, who had been bullied. Instead, I concentrated on my research and teaching, focusing on inspiring students to appreciate an avant-garde movement that welcomed women and writers and artists from a variety of national, social, racial, and ethnic backgrounds. I wanted them to see the links between the young men and women who created the surrealist movement in Paris in the 1920s and 1930s and the anti-war movements that swept Europe and the United States in the 1960s and 1970s, along with calls to end colonialism and support civil rights and women's rights.

Six years after I was promoted and had submitted my dossier for promotion to the rank of professor, I was asked by my provost at Dartmouth, who had been my associate dean during my first failed attempt at promotion to the rank of associate professor with tenure, to lead the search for a new dean of the libraries. In retrospect, I believe it was his way of introducing me to how a university actually works by introducing me to colleagues who were essential to the university's functioning and yet unknown to me because they were outside my field. As one humanist to another, he was mentoring me by showing his confidence in my ability to operate effectively beyond the classroom and my department. When I asked advice from my current associate dean, she made the comment that if I succeeded with the search, it would "make my career," and she turned out to be right.

That search for the dean of the libraries provided me with a greater appreciation for the colleagues I had in the library and also allowed me to lead a group of colleagues the way I lead my seminars: by giving voice to all, as equitably as possible. I made sure we gathered input from multiple constituents on campus, starting with the library staff, the faculty, and students. The chosen candidate was truly a group choice, made after extensive consultation. I had learned a lot from the feminist scholars who had hired me in 1992 and had shown me that it is possible to lead in a way that empowers the collective while simultaneously honoring individual voices. About the time we succeeded in hiring our top choice, I received the news that my application for promotion had been successful.

The following year I was surprised to learn that my colleagues had recommended me to be the next department chair. I was bemused to recognize that my effort to be friendly to everyone throughout the two difficult years I spent as an associate professor without tenure might have been more effective than I had intended. It had begun as a mode of protection, as a way of acting on the two mantras that sustained me—never let them see you sweat and living well is the best revenge. My goal had simply been to make myself less angry and to learn how to live with my colleagues so that I could do my work without bitterness. I had never intended to campaign for the position of chair! Nonetheless, once I agreed to step into that role I recognized it as an opportunity to follow the example of the feminist colleagues who had chaired the department before me.

Under the leadership of Mary Jean Green and Lynn Higgins, every member of the department, no matter how junior, had a voice. They showed me what feminist values look like in university administration: the power to make sure that information was broadly shared, to make decisions as a group and not behind closed doors with limited consultation, to shut down end-runs, to communicate all information coming from the higher administration, to pursue policies for evaluation of junior colleagues that allowed them to have input in the process, and to establish roles for junior faculty on all departmental committees. They had modeled for me a feminist style of leadership rooted in their belief in the collective good that I resolved to emulate.

The summer before I started chairing, I enrolled in a seminar for new chairs of English and Foreign Languages and Literatures, run by the Modern Language Association (MLA). A chair of English I met over dinner suggested I interview each one of my colleagues about their expectations by asking them four questions—"How do you see the department now? Where do you think it should be in five years? Whom should we hire to reach that goal? What role would you like to play?" to which I added a fifth question: "Tell me about your research," since I realized I did not know as much as I'd like about their scholarly work. I learned a lot about my colleagues from this approach and discovered I was surprised by some of their answers and pleased that some of my quieter colleagues were interested in greater engagement.

My education in feminist leadership continued with my service on the MLA's Committee on the Status of Women in the Profession (CSWP), during which we launched the project that would eventually be published in 2009 as *Standing Still, The Associate Professor Survey*.[1] I learned a lot from my fellow female humanists on the committee, especially Michelle Massé, who has a chapter in this volume, about the benefit of individualized mentoring for female academics after tenure, along with strategic advice for planning for promotion to the rank of professor. Too many female academics "stand still" as associate professors; we wanted to encourage them to advance in their careers and narrow the pay gap between male and female academics as a result. The research we did on the CSWP taught me to be more attentive to my own female colleagues, to their challenges and experiences, and to recognize the extent to which existing administrative structures in our universities have been built on white male models. The CSWP reinforced for me the importance of supporting and encouraging my female colleagues and colleagues of color, which began to make leadership more attractive as a way of validating the experiences of my peers. I began to understand better the story one mentor had told me about a conversation she had had with a close friend after she had been invited to serve as associate dean, during which her friend had exclaimed as a teasing challenge: "If we're going to work for the darn places, we might as well run them!"

Nonetheless, it was only when I was elected to serve on the search committee for the next dean of the faculty of arts & sciences at Dartmouth, where the deanship is an internal position, that I began to understand what deans did and, to my surprise, their work sounded interesting, in particular, how wide-ranging the projects were in the dean's office, how supportive of faculty research and teaching deans can be, how much like me the deans we interviewed were. I recognized that all the associate deans with whom I'd worked personally were colleagues I liked and trusted as well as admired. I was happy to be part of a committee that recommended a woman to serve as the first female dean of the faculty of arts and sciences. When she called to invite me to serve with her as an associate dean, I was less surprised than I might have been, having learned from the search what kinds of qualifications were needed and, after reviewing my options, I agreed.

I had learned from my year as chair and my service on the CSWP that it can be meaningful for women on the faculty to see women in leadership positions. I had also learned that women were not in more leadership positions partly because of a lack of self-confidence similar to the lack of confidence we sometimes see in female students in mixed classrooms. I didn't want a negative response to the dean's invitation to be motivated by fear. Instead, I recognized the chance to play an active role in mentoring peers and to have greater confidence in *their* abilities, and so I began to see that taking on a leadership role as a woman could help me grow in ways I had not anticipated and simultaneously allow me to enact my feminist values in new and unexpected ways.

When I became an academic, I had never imagined I could turn fifty and learn a whole new job. I always thought I would keep growing while doing the same things I had done from the start—research and teaching. When I returned to graduate school at age thirty, I had finally found my life's work—work that never bored me, unlike the string of jobs in publishing I had held throughout my twenties, jobs that always started out well but that had eventually became repetitive. I was shocked in my late twenties to realize that, despite my valued independence, I had expected that the course of my life would be determined by finding my life's partner in college, the way my mother had, but that hadn't happened and didn't seem likely as my thirtieth birthday came into view. It was only in my late twenties that I truly understood the importance of meaningful work. I was gratified to have finally found it in academia, just as my mother eventually found it with the law degree she earned the year I would have, had I listened to my father's advice and taken the LSATs (Law School Admission Test) in my senior year of college. I recognized that the step into a position of authority would allow me to redefine what that concept meant to me. Instead of imagining filling my authoritarian father's shoes—which was not appealing—I could imagine wearing a different kind of shoe.

My five years in the Dartmouth dean's office as associate dean for the arts & humanities were challenging and exciting—challenging, because colleagues I thought I knew suddenly seemed to expect me to make choices that favored them; exciting, because I had a fantastic group of new colleagues. I had never worked in such a supportive environment. My fellow deans and administrators wanted only the best for me; they saw my success as their success. Having reached my goal of adding the "arts" to the division title in the first few months, changing it from the "humanities" to the "arts and humanities," I set out to learn as much as I could about the best ways to promote the arts and humanities within the university, as well as the status of women in my assigned departments. I had not previously realized how many initiatives start in the dean's office. I was thrilled to join the effort of my dean to work on correcting the significant gender pay gap that had existed for years in arts and sciences.

Deans have a platform to advocate for the liberal arts. I believe I've learned from experience that all of us who work in higher education should have a stake in how it is practiced, a voice in how it is administered. I had not realized how much strategic behind-the-scenes group planning and brainstorming deans do as part of the work of shared governance. As associate dean I was in a position to introduce colleagues to one another, to support the efforts of the university museum, performing arts center, and library to improve their facilities, to meet alumni serving on various Boards, and to raise money for faculty projects across the arts and humanities. My predecessor turned out to be right—alumni donors were a lot like my students, only a little older. Throughout my first five years, I also kept myself grounded by continuing to do the work of the faculty I was in charge of supervising, namely, by continuing to do my research by making time for it during the early morning hours.

After five years, I was convinced I was ready to return to full-time research and teaching, when the chance to interview for the deanship at William & Mary arose in the fall of 2011. When I met the search committee, I was impressed with them and I realized that I had experience that could be useful in this new environment. I was also excited at the prospect of working at a public university after many years in private institutions and at collaborating specifically with the faculty I'd met through the search. I was intrigued by the chance to get to know and support faculty from all the departments and interdisciplinary programs across the arts and sciences, beyond my familiar sphere of the arts and humanities.

When I started as dean at William & Mary in 2012, I was able to oversee a faculty-driven initiative to update general education that had begun six months prior to my arrival; this effort was helped significantly by a Mellon Foundation grant I secured in collaboration with my fellow deans, including a talented grant-writer. The COLL (for College) curriculum had been created by an extensive and inclusive faculty committee co-led by Teresa Longo, a faculty leader I was lucky to work with in a variety of capacities, and required a lengthy approval process. I learned at William & Mary how important it is to consult as many groups as possible, to an even greater extent than at my previous private university. These consultations took more time than I was accustomed to taking and stretched my feminist values of collective decision-making, but resulted in better decisions. We initially faced opposition to the new curriculum from within the faculty, which required strategic effort on the part of a variety of groups who supported the process—including the four associate deans, known at William & Mary as "contact" deans, who worked closely with me, and the elected Faculty Affairs Committee, and Educational Policy Committee. Then, once the majority of the faculty had voted in favor of proceeding with the proposed new curriculum, we faced opposition from conversative alumni groups, who falsely claimed we were abandoning traditional subjects in our effort to support innovative cross-disciplinary approaches to teaching. That we launched the COLL curriculum successfully in the fall of 2015 felt like a true triumph of collaboration.

I learned to resist my natural wish to be liked in favor of doing my best to gain respect. When challenged, I framed my answers in terms of accountability—my own and that of my team, but also that of all the faculty—to the shared goal that united us of providing students with the best possible education. I benefitted greatly from serving on the Board of the Council of Colleges of Arts and Sciences (CCAS) for eight years, as the dean at the host institution for the organization. I learned and lived the extent to which deans can play a key role in instituting social change within an institution.

Having discovered how exciting it can be to oversee a university's academic curriculum—one of the principal responsibilities for a dean of arts and sciences—I turned to other projects such as collaboratively planning and implementing our comprehensive action plan for diversity and inclusion, and organizing its annual update. I was also able to support a faculty initiative to improve working conditions for lecturers by integrating them more fully into academic life and implementing a process for promotion to senior lecturer. Improving working conditions and regularizing pay increases for lecturers accorded well with my feminist values since many of our lecturer colleagues were women. (In one memorable conversation with a male chair, which included myself and the female supervisory "contact dean" for the department in question, we pointed out the inequity of the visiting assistant professors, who were all male, earning more and teaching less than the female lecturers who were consistently highly reviewed and taught all the essential introductory courses for less pay; he was genuinely surprised by this observation.) For faculty on the tenure track, I sought to motivate their desire for promotion to the rank of professor by increasing the salary bump at the point of promotion from $500 to $5000. Simply adding a zero made a difference. I met regularly with faculty coming up for tenure to encourage them to think of it as a step along a dynamic trajectory that extends well beyond the next promotion, partly based on what I had learned from the MLA's CSWP, which had shown me how women tend to lag behind their male peers. I told junior faculty the story of a (female) friend of mine's comment upon receiving promotion—"I just don't want them telling me what to do anymore," with reference to her senior (mostly male) departmental colleagues.

Deans can set many goals such as supporting graduate students by advocating for increased stipends and research funds; promoting global education by supporting study abroad options; regularizing compensation for faculty leaders and making that scale of compensation public knowledge; establishing a system for equitable distribution of prizes and fellowships; systematically investigating complaints of sexual harassment in partnership with the Office of Compliance; finding funding for new programming, such as a William & Mary faculty-led program that helps first-generation and transfer students to succeed by pairing them with research-active faculty in their first years. Equity is an ongoing struggle for a dean; it is also an important feminist value.

Advocating for equity and accountability in every domain can be hard but one of the most rewarding efforts available to those who enter administration.

Together with a dean team of four "contact" deans, the director of finance, the director for advancement, and the director of communications, we established a clear chain of communication that promoted transparency. We encouraged faculty to talk to their chairs, rather than going straight to the dean, and chairs to talk to their "contact" deans, again, rather than going straight to the dean. We made sure that the chair or program director for any colleague who came to the dean's office was included in that chain of communication. To the initial complaint that I was not as accessible to faculty as my predecessor, I pointed out that this way I was accessible to more faculty since five deans who are in good communication with one another can talk to more faculty more of the time than just one.

As dean, I sought to emulate my role models, including the first female dean of the faculty at Dartmouth who had hired me into dean's office. Like Carol Folt, now president of the University of Southern California, I sought to delegate as much as possible, partly to distribute authority and leadership and partly to train the deans who worked under me so that they would be prepared, the way I had been by Carol, to step into the top jobs. Carol taught me to trust in teamwork, to work with my team and take the time I needed to make decisions that would have an impact on others. For someone always eager to cross off the next thing on my to-do list, this was a tough lesson but one that paid back with results every time I listened to my inner voice reminding me to slow down. I also benefitted from the opportunity to participate in programs offered by the Harvard Graduate School of Education for university administrators, where I met my co-editor Shaily Menon, as well as Tim Hall and Sheryl Fontaine, both of whom contributed to this volume. These programs offered tangible strategies for problem-solving rooted in basic self-care: kindness to others starts with kindness to oneself. The Harvard Institute for Management and Leadership in Education, which had been recommended to me by my CCAS mentor, and the Harvard Building Inner Strengths of Leaders Program focused on mindfulness, both reinforced the advice I had been given when I started as associate dean from my predecessor—to make time for myself, for my health and my scholarship. Deans are caretakers of the faculty and their staff. To nourish others, we need to nourish ourselves. I'm grateful to have had this lesson reinforced as I faced some of the inevitable pushback that comes with leading change, including from those who, based on past experience, expected to receive favors by extending friendship to me.

I left the deanship two years ago for a convergence of reasons. First, I had accomplished what I set out to do—to establish greater accountability, equity, and transparency in the running of arts & sciences and to lead the process of adopting the new COLL general education curriculum. Second, I was beginning to look enviously at the faculty I passed daily on my walks across campus, wishing I were in their shoes. Then a new president was installed who made it clear she wanted to appoint new deans to the five deanships at our university, once she had hired a new provost. It was as if I had become invisible in plain sight, silenced, after having been seen and heard for seven years. Two of us stepped down a year later, at the outset of the pandemic, in the new provost's first year; another followed last year; the fifth will retire at the end of this year. Stepping down was hard, just as stepping up had been at the outset. I found it hard to say goodbye to my team and staff, to stop the forward momentum of the previous eight years.

As it happened, my fears—that I would regret my wish to return to the faculty and that I would miss my daily life as dean—turned out to be unwarranted. Handing over my responsibilities to my successor came as a relief because I was more ready than I had realized, especially in the early months of the pandemic. I was still dean when we switched to remote teaching in mid-March 2020. We quickly partnered with Information Technology on setting up seminars for faculty who wanted support for their (in many cases first) remote teaching experience, and we initiated planning for new budget cuts, in order to make it through the loss of university revenue incurred by the pandemic. My successor was eager to dig into the budget whereas I was ready to let that responsibility go, having written multiple proposals for budget increases—to accommodate the new curriculum—and inevitable cuts over the years. I recognized myself at the outset of my deanship in her energetic enthusiasm and realized how fortuitous the timing of my departure was. The coach I had hired to help me with public speaking—a duty I had never enjoyed at an institution where I was responsible for leading faculty meetings on a monthly basis—proved to be the perfect person to help me through my two years of transition: out of my job as dean and into my new job on the faculty. My department has been lovely to me; my students inspiring; and the chance to teach what I love—surrealism in literature, art, and life, and second-wave Francophone feminism—has been more rewarding than I could have imagined. I even enjoyed remote teaching during the pandemic! Having monitored the faculty seminars organized by colleagues in IT at the pandemic's outset while I was still dean, I was quick to sign myself up four months later for training that helped me navigate what might otherwise have been a bewildering experience after 13 years outside of the classroom, aside from occasional independent studies. While I can truly say that I loved my job as dean (the rumor that taking a role in administration involves crossing over to the dark side is greatly exaggerated), I have had no regrets stepping away and moving forward.

I will conclude with an anecdote and an observation. In my twenties, I had four jobs in journal, magazine, and book publishing in New York and Colorado. The last of these was at a big enough press to have a head of Human Resources, who invited me to tell him about my vision for my future in his modest office at the center of the building. No one had ever asked me that a question before. In addition to outlining my ambitions in publishing, I commented that I was interested in improving working conditions for my colleagues. I hadn't yet figured out that my growing feminist perspective was at the root of this wish. I have remembered this conversation throughout my years as a dean because, in a way, my work in administration allowed me to act on this early career desire. No life experience goes unwasted, ultimately, and this is perhaps the greatest lesson from my story.

Notes

[1] Modern Language Association (MLA). Website publication date, 27 April, 2009. https://www.mla.org/About-Us/Governance/Committees/Committee-Listings/Professional-Issues/Committee-on-Women-Gender-and-Sexuality-in-the-Profession/Standing-Still-The-Associate-Professor-Survey.

Three

Narrating Administration

Michelle A. Massé
Louisiana State University

Abstract

In "Narrating Administration" I focus upon storytelling as a key way in which we explain the paths that lead us to administration, and upon the important ways in which women in particular are rewriting the tales they tell themselves and others. I first make some general observations about the ur-narrative of administration, then tell a short story about my own development as a feminist administrator, and finally analyze basic elements of that fiction: setting, character, point of view, theme, plot, and closure. What I most emphasize is how integral revision is to administration and how vital boundary-crossing—of genres, of fields, of commitments, of identity itself—is to its healthy growth. In addition, I argue that the protagonist-administrators of the future will minimize individualist prominence and increasingly articulate their leadership through relationship, community, and mentoring.

Keywords: Age Studies, associate professor project, *Bildungsroman*, character, closure, collaboration, graduate school, *David Copperfield*, Charles Dickens, Disability Studies, feminism, Feminist Theory and Criticism series, fiction, first-generation, focalization, genre, gender, journey, inclusion, narrative theory, plot, point-of-view, setting

***

In their introduction to this volume, Kate Conley and Shaily Menon emphasize "the power of storytelling." As someone who works in narrative theory, I heartily endorse that statement. The stories we tell non-academics to explain what we do as administrators are crucial in creating shared realities. The stories we tell ourselves and others within academic communities, however, are still more vital as we weave and re-weave the plots that explain how and why we got to where we are as administrators.

In this essay, I am first going to make some general observations about the ur-narrative of administration, then tell a short story about my own developmental arc as a feminist administrator, and finally analyze basic elements of that fiction:

setting, character, point of view, theme, plot, and closure. That story might have had a different organization ten years ago; ten years from now it may have yet another. What I want most to emphasize in this version, however, is how integral revision is to administration and how vital boundary-crossing - of genres, of fields, of commitments, of identity itself - is to its healthy growth.

My dissertation many years ago was on narcissism and the *Bildungsroman*, or novel of development. My interest in how key psychoanalytic issues shape genre and gender led me to explore the rich ways in which both healthy and pathological narcissism are intertwined with what we would now call entitlement and privilege by dint of sex, race, and class. We are all familiar with the time-honed core plot of the *Bildungsroman*. Indeed, the most familiar form, in tracing the linear transition from innocence to experience, from country to city, from false choices to right ones for work and love, almost always foregrounding a central character who is (or believes him/her self to be) what Freud called an "exception," in fact works as well for the road to the deanship as it does for most other journeys. In its most traditional form, this administrative *Bildung* traces the step-by-step progression from being a director of undergraduate studies, say, through department chair, to associate dean or dean, and perhaps even finally to the roles of provost or president.

That linear journey is still followed by some, but it's not the tale I want to tell. That "once upon a time" narrative will not be the road most taken for administrators of the future. Its monolithic narrowing of vistas, even while the traveler is ostensibly scaling new heights, means casting aside much in order to climb quickly. Think of the familiar sardonic observation about "going over to the dark side," of supposedly leaving behind the triadic professorial responsibilities that have shaped us through research, teaching, and service. As the plot above also suggests, part of what also gets jettisoned in this tired variant are the relationships that have shaped years of professional identity so that the individual faculty member, shorn of non-essentials, can become that brooding presence, the administrator, who determines salaries, policies, and recognition.

The new story today's administrators are writing is one in which we willingly carry a lot with us to the dean's office: our engagements with multiple communities, our newly complicated understandings of pedagogy, the research skills that let us investigate problems rather than assuming received truths are correct answers. We carry our beliefs in inclusion; we carry our commitments to collaborative futures; as caregivers, we carry our old and our young. We cross boundaries and then re-draw them. All of this may make our journeys slower and our detours more frequent, and our decisions about destinations and time of arrival more flexible.

I always encourage graduate students and junior colleagues to strike out in new directions, and to remember that neither their departments nor their colleges are the world. Faculty working with colleagues from across the campus in programs such as Women's and Gender Studies (WGS), African and African-American Studies, Asian Studies, LGBTQ+, Disability Studies, or Age Studies, to name just a few, exemplify one effective way to assure that one is never "home alone" and isolated in the "home" department. Increasingly too, the roles that prepare faculty to administer also prepare them to minister: we indeed learn how to manage, distribute, and organize, but also how to care for and attend to. Administrative roles in non-singular units encourage faculty to recognize campuses as multi-disciplinary organisms from their administrative first. Directors of labs, service-learning programs, community outreach initiatives, writing across the curriculum, international student mentoring, etc. are increasingly recognized as colleagues whose expertise is as complicated, as necessary, and as generously contributing to the community as that of a department chair.

My Story

My interest in the structure of universities and of "the profession" is part and parcel of my own absorption in interdisciplinary thought. I've worked with hybrid methodologies such as gender theory, psychoanalysis, and cultural studies in my scholarship and my teaching, but further crossing the boundaries within the traditional triad of research, teaching, and service has led to my most fruitful thinking. My work as a series editor for the State University of New York's (SUNY) Feminist Theory and Criticism series, my research, and my teaching enrich my administrative practice, just as my administrative jobs have generated new ideas in the classroom and the library. For example, my co-edited collection, *Over Ten Million Served* (2010), brings scholarship to bear upon the gendered role of service in universities' silent economies. Another co-edited project, *Staging Women's Lives in Academia* (2017), draws upon Age Studies as well to consider the often uneasy disjuncture between "life stages" in personal and professional lives for women. Whether I am teaching seminars about pedagogy or the university as an institution, writing a psychoanalytic analysis of administrative culture, or researching the implications of policy decisions, I find it crucial to check the received truth of each sphere against insights from the others.

As a junior faculty member, however, I identified what I was doing to establish curricula and policy as "administration" slowly and reluctantly. As a working-class, first-generation college graduate on one side, and high-school graduate on the other, I never doubted but that I was building and directing, but I was reluctant to cross the line to what I perceived as management. Yet, as I have stated elsewhere, my sense of leadership was profoundly shaped by nuns and nurses, neither of whom ever eschewed authority. What I *did* recognize from an early point was that I liked designing courses and curricula, and that equitable policies and procedures help us to achieve what we want to do more quickly, and let us do so in a good mood to boot. Since graduate school, I accordingly helped to develop or revise six programs as a member of their executive (or equivalent) committees. While still untenured, I became the founding director of my current school's Women's and Gender Studies program. And I have served—in most cases gladly—on a myriad of university, professional, and community committees that I believed would help to make the ideals of academic community a reality. The achievements of numerous university-wide commissions and task forces that addressed topics such as long-range planning, multiculturalism and diversity, graduate education, the status of academic ranks, sexual harassment, the status of women, and post-tenure review have changed the campus climate at my school significantly, as has my role as an advisor for the formation of interdisciplinary programs such as International Studies, Jewish Studies, and African-American Studies. National work, whether as a consultant for other schools, in service to groups such as the Council of Graduate Schools or the Modern Language Association (MLA) or in helping to launch the Age Studies organization, is similarly an important part of administrative community engagement for me.

For example, as dean of the graduate school, and as part of my goal to wean it away from being a service-defined unit to one that also embraced the more capacious challenges of graduate studies, I inaugurated a three-week, five-hour daily summer institute on the Future of Graduate Studies, a Grad Gen 1 group for first-generation graduate students, a campus-wide voluntary mentoring program for students and faculty cross-colleges, and an associate professor project to support graduate faculty making the often-neglected transition from associate to full. I've used similar strategies for other posts, whether forming a new chairs' mentoring system as acting associate dean of the College of Arts and Sciences, inaugurating a major project on associate professors at the MLA, bringing undergraduate and graduate students together in workshops while directing WGS or organizing diversity recruiting workshops and Alternative Academic (Alt-Ac) panels for graduate students.

As you might expect from the above, from my having served repeatedly on groups such as the Faculty Senate and Senate Grievance Committee, and from my involvement in activities such as presentations about mentoring graduate students, the future of higher education, and the feminization of contingent labor, I am passionate about equity and open process. Becoming an administrator is not a disavowal of those commitments, however, but rather the concentrated attempt to find the best arenas through which to effect change.

As I finish my short story about my own development as an administrator, I hope that many of you have already identified a narrative problem: the "I, I, I" of first-person narration is at odds with the reality of governance and program development, which only a "we" can and should generate. There's also a suspicious smoothness of plot trajectory from my receiving the PhD to the happy ending of becoming the interim vice provost for graduate studies and dean of the graduate school that belies a path in which I in fact (usually voluntarily) cycled in and out of administration. In the final section of this essay, I'd like for us to consider moving inductively from specific examples such as my own or those in the ur-story in order to analyze the elements of our general fictions about administration. By shaping a theory of administration, we can map a journey to better individual and institutional futures.

Setting

As an element of fiction, setting's concreteness can make it seem the element least subject to interpretation, most easy to skip over as a given as we eye more inviting analytic challenges. Setting isn't just geographical and architectural, however; it also involves time and social context. We're familiar with the institutional settings in which we live, which come to seem "natural" and which can thus generate assumptions about others'. Look back at my personal story, for example. I never say that I work at a university, but my reference to graduate students (as well as to being the dean of the graduate school) suggests that that is the case. Had I said "doctoral students," as I considered doing, then I would have narrowed my peer institutions to about 10% of higher education institutions. I also never say "United States" in my construction of the ur-narrative, but surely the list of interdisciplinary programs I list would suggest this to many readers. Our assumptions about setting can generate blithe fallacies that distort effective policy and planning. If the peer institutes and the practices I uncritically accept as gold standard spring from a privileged undergraduate experience, for instance (mine don't), I risk setting goals and expectations that are ill-suited to the realities of the present. We all know George Santayana's maxim: "Those who cannot remember the past are condemned to repeat it." Those who only recognize the past are also condemned to repeat it, however. Idealizing either the past or the future of a school ignores the pressing realities of the present, whether manifested through curriculum or physical plant.

Character

At the beginning of Charles Dickens's *David Copperfield*, David wonders "Whether I shall turn out to be the hero of my own life."[1] What's sometimes called "protagonism" to describe the centrality of one figure in a story articulates a basic wish we all have. Yet, as I suggest above, the "I, I, I" of first-personal narrative is at odds with the reality of worlds that contain other characters as fully rounded as ourselves. Power or authority can help to sustain the illusions of protagonism because as deans we can hire or appoint many of our associates. If I surround myself with others who agree with me or who are like me, then I've basically created secondary or flat characters who function as attributes or mirrors of my fully-developed self. As a feminist committed to inclusion, collaboration, and activism, I've often been mortified to look at the first list I draw up for committee members, say, and realize how predictable it is. Time and again I have to think about what the unspoken parameters are for such lists, and question when and how I learned my exclusionary and inclusionary practices. One specific positive example comes from my graduate education. I never questioned being included in social events at faculty members' houses, whether dinner parties or larger social gatherings. I was therefore startled when, after hosting my first large gathering as a faculty member at a new school, a number of colleagues commented upon my including graduate students as guests. Look at your own invitation lists, whether for parties or task forces, and ask yourself why someone is or isn't the character you want in this scene.

Conversely, remembering that I'm that flat character, The Dean, in someone else's story can be soothing at 2:00 in the morning when I'm pondering how anyone could ever have said or done such-and-such a thing to fully round Me. We need to be careful about invoking this narcotic reminder too often, however, because saying "They don't really know Me" and are responding to a character function can lead quickly to also deciding that "They don't know the real story." (See "listening" and "plot.")

Being a round character, and expanding the cast of round characters are crucial for all administrators, whether including non-tenure-track faculty and graduate students in committees, associate professors on key committees, or staff on task forces.

Point of View/Focalization

Point of view, more often called "focalization" now, is closely allied to character. The first-person point of view I refer to above is one example, in which the person who gets to tell the story holds the stage. There are other kinds of structures, however, in which the person telling the story is the channel for letting many other peoples' stories be told. This, I think, is ultimately my own administrative goal. I certainly don't want to silence my own voice, but I also don't want it to be the only voice. Listening, rather than talking, is crucial and (for me at least), a hard-earned skill. In administration, as in teaching, it's often obvious that you can get things done more quickly by doing them yourself—

and it's almost always a bad idea. I don't shy away from taking responsibility, or the hard realities of personnel and procedural decisions that rightfully end up on the dean's desk. But I also know that ideas don't "take" unless the members of a group know that the decision is theirs also. I always try to seek other points of focalization. Asking for ideas from colleagues with very different disciplinary perspectives, or from colleagues with similar positions on other campuses, almost always leads to thoughtful and generous responses. Here again, though, research can amplify those other voices, whether found in *Inside Higher Ed* and *The Chronicle of Higher Education* columns, or the enormously helpful list-servs and resources maintained by professional organizations such as the Council for Colleges of Arts & Sciences, the Council of Graduate Schools, and the Association of American Colleges and Universities (AAC&U).

Theme

Themes answer the crucial question "So what?" This simple and confoundedly hard question is central to every administrative initiative. A bad theme is like a bad mission statement, which we have surely all read (and perhaps even written)—so cosmic, so over-reaching, that no one can dissent from it, but neither can anyone get anything done by following it. Themes can also be very allied to what we might call the thesis or argument of a story, when we try to figure out what it all means. I have all too often found myself floundering in answering that question, in effect sputtering "Well. . . . Well. . . . Just *because!*" Because it's always been done that way, because everyone else does it, because the report is due, darn it. But as administrators we must have themes: not twenty of them, and not a monomaniacal single vision, but themes. Where do you want your program to be in five years? Where do *you* want to be in five years? Why? What are the stages that will lead to those destinations? There are most certainly days when the only "Why?" being asked is through a howl of anguish after six Zoom meetings or at the announcement of a new platform that is heralded as the best thing since sliced bread. At some point, though—and that point will vary according to our own organizational habits—we need to re-articulate and re-calibrate our themes. I have colleagues who use white boards in their offices that specify goals for the week, the month, and the semester. I know others who have astonishing (to me) color-coded priority lists. Stopping to ask yourself where you are on last semester's (or last year's) top-priority goal is a good exercise in either saying that it isn't a goal anymore, or that it's a key theme to which you must return.

Plot

Plot is the sequence of events that makes up our stories. Not surprisingly, as we know from our sometimes-paranoid (and sometimes not) suspicions about others' plotting, conflict is also integral to plot. There is conflict, tension increases, and then there is resolution. There is often also an implied causality, often retrospective or teleological, in plot, in which we re-read the beginning so that it coheres with the ending. "How I became the Dean" or "How I met my life partner" are often narratives in which other narrative paths are sheared away, or minimized to a single false start before The Right Path was found. For administrators, the negative connotations of plot and conflict can become dominant. Never ascribing to malice what can be ascribed to incompetence or ignorance is an important mantra that prevents your entering into conspiracy plots. The faculty member who asks "Why haven't we received raises in four years?" may not have a clue about which part of the budget you control, any more than those who suspect that you have a bucket of money in your bottom desk drawer. Engaging—or creating—such plot conflict is not useful on multiple fronts, although working to assure that everyone has accurate information is. What's more important is plotting your own path. You don't want to rely upon your own *deus ex machina*, or god from the machine. Saying "The provost made me do it" is not an answer or, if it is the only answer you can give, it's worth thinking about "Theme" again. Create your own positive plot.

Closure

As surely as we all want to believe that we will be the heroines and heroes of our own administrative lives, we also want to believe that we will live happily ever after. Thinking through the personal and professional themes of our own lives may also mean that we re-define those themes, though. "Closure" suggests a door shutting, options closed, and the suspension of time, even with the hallowed happy ending. Closure is also one of the most ambiguous of terms. If new chapters or doors opening are often ascribed, particularly by women and members of under-represented groups, as due to chance, luck, or good fortune rather than one's own merit, so too their closing may be remembered as books slammed shut or doors barred by others. Choosing one's own closure, like choosing one's theme, is vital for any administrator. If you want to leave the position or the school, despite being wildly successful in the job, think about what's holding you back. Is there a perception of failure because of the traditional linear plot of progress through academic ranks and administration? In the edited collection on life stages I referred to above, as well as in several panels on similar topics, the rarest (and hardest to gather) narratives were those from faculty who left academia after tenure because of their seeming repudiation of what should have been deemed "success." They re-defined their plots, themes, and characters, however. Refusing to continue as chair of the department is recognizable; deciding not to continue as dean or provost often generates an astonishment similar to that of refusing tenure. Recognize that your decision may signal a new chapter or even a sequel, and that you're the one writing it.

In this essay's own closure, let me say that I hope that every reader will craft her or his own administrative narrative to help create not just a fiction, but a reality, in which administrative and faculty stories open, rather than close, new chapters for others to read and to write.

Notes

[1] Charles Dickens, *David Copperfield*, Revised Edition (London: Penguin Books, 2014), 13.

Four

Discovering a Calling:
How I became a Dean

Timothy D. Hall

Samford University

Abstract

This essay reflects upon the author's surprising experience of transition from regular faculty to the dean's chair as a process of self-discovery and reframing of university administration as a deeply human role dedicated to making the university community better for faculty and students alike. The past fifteen years of experience in academic leadership called out previously unexercised skills in organization, analysis, and problem-solving that helped make first my department, then my college a more effective and congenial place to work. This experience has also revealed administrative work to be anything but impersonal or soulless. Rather, it is a deeply social and humane calling, one that requires the academic leader to develop strong personal relationships and partnerships across a diversity of disciplines and often-competing interests to unite colleagues around a compelling common vision.

Keywords: administration, assistant dean, associate dean, assessment program, budget, Central Michigan University, COVID-19, chair, faith-based institution, History, Howard College of Arts & Sciences, interim, leadership, mentoring, Pandemic Response Team, pre-tenure faculty, professional development, program assessment, Reiksuniversiteit Groningen, Samford University, service, teamwork, Zoom

***

"You know what they say about an associate dean," asked a colleague at a dinner party not long after I had accepted an interim appointment to that role. I didn't. He grinned and went on, "a mouse in training to become a rat."

The joke annoyed my wife Sheree, who was sitting next to me at the dinner party, but it resonated with my own ambivalence about my new title and duties. I shared the usual suspicions of my unionized faculty colleagues about the motives and goals of university administration, perhaps especially since we had only recently emerged from an especially contentious season of contract negotiations. I was also torn between the time-consuming burden of administration and the prospect of having more time for teaching and scholarship after having served as department chair for the previous six years. I had enjoyed serving as department chair and felt reasonably happy with my achievements in that role, but the previous year's duties had begun to feel less like interesting problems and challenges and more like familiar routines. By the end of that year, I was glad that my department limited service as chair to no more than two three-year terms and that someone else could step in for a rotation at the helm. A semester of teaching abroad at the Reiksuniversiteit Groningen in the Netherlands during my first year of return to faculty life had already given me a stimulating new classroom experience while helping to jump-start my scholarly projects, reminding me afresh of why I had pursued academic life in the first place. Then came the invitation to step into a newly-created assistant deanship in Central Michigan University's college of Humanities and Social and Behavioral Sciences just as the semester abroad was nearing completion. Dean Pamela Gates gave me the final weeks of that semester to consider. I took all the time she gave me to weigh the pros and cons. When I returned to the U.S. I accepted "just to try it out for a year," and my career path changed.

I have known some administrators who actually entered graduate school with the goal of winning an administrative post by the time they were forty, but that had never been my aim. My wife sometimes reminds me that shortly after we met in college, I told her that I hoped to become a university professor. I received tenure in the Department of History at CMU almost twenty years later and planned to spend the rest of my career between the classroom and the study. Shortly after receiving promotion to full professor, however, my department elected me chair. I expected it to be only a temporary interruption: I would serve my allotted two terms in the role and then return to faculty.

Once in the role, however, I discovered that I possessed leadership abilities that I had never recognized. Chief among them turned out to be an ability to reach across divisions and help my colleagues work together toward shared goals. When I stepped into the chair's office, the warfare among factions prompted me to pray St. Francis's prayer, "Lord, make me an instrument of your peace." Advice from a seasoned chair early in my first term—"Tim, remember that you are chair of the *whole* department"—proved key to my peacemaking efforts. The skill of listening that I had learned from my wife served the effort as I learned to seek out colleagues and have frank, open conversations with them about their hopes and concerns for the department. By the end of my first three-year term, we had together managed to work beyond our differences and had launched a new long-term plan to strengthen and expand our graduate program to include new international partners. By the end of my second term, we had strengthened our existing partnership while adding three new ones and had implemented a much-needed reform of the undergraduate curriculum.

I also discovered that I enjoyed both the strategic and personal aspects of administrative work. I found that the chair's office gave me the influence to effect changes in policy and priorities that had hampered department's effectiveness for a long time. I discovered a knack for identifying structural deficiencies in our management of our affairs and for devising workable remedies. Our undergraduate curriculum and advising needed better coordination, for example, and the remedy was the appointment of a faculty coordinator who was interested and motivated to manage that function. I also discovered that applying the influence to achieve such solutions was one of the most enjoyable aspects of administration since it meant building collegial relationships. This meant a lot of purposeful socializing—going to lunches, meeting colleagues at the brew pub, hosting department get-togethers at my house. In those gatherings the women and men with whom I worked and planned could forge the whole department into a working team. We were even able to hold at least two overnight departmental retreats during my tenure where whole families convened to enjoy informal time together and spouses took the kids while the mothers and fathers joined us for planning sessions. In these collegial settings we strengthened friendships, explored solutions to departmental problems, and hatched plans to address them. It also meant working with those colleagues as teammates on the solutions we had agreed upon.

Professional development and mentoring of junior colleagues proved another rewarding aspect of my administrative role. In the course of my six years in the department, I oversaw the hiring of nearly half its faculty. Each of these new colleagues needed orientation to the university's tenure and promotion process and the resources the department and college had provided to help them with achievement in each area. The responsibility for mentorship did not fall fully to me, of course; all senior members of the department took on a share of the task. Some fulfilled these duties better than others, however, and most junior faculty raised at least a few questions that required a response from me. I learned to welcome these opportunities to converse with junior colleagues, learn a little more about their stories, and offer them assistance toward understanding and making progress toward their career goals. Several of them became good friends and collaborators on various department projects, and I remain in contact with some of them to this day.

By the time I had completed my second term as chair and been term-limited out of further service in that role, I had come to realize that administration was far more than paper-pushing. It offered an opportunity to become a builder of a team of talented colleagues whom I could rally to build meaningful programs for our students and of the systems and procedures that would make them work efficiently and effectively. I found the work challenging, exciting, and rewarding, even though it was different than the path of teaching and scholarship that I had always planned to follow. I had also come to view the dean and associate dean not as adversaries, but as dedicated and concerned colleagues ready to partner with me and my faculty to make us better. When Dean Gates invited me to become an assistant dean in my college, the groundwork had been prepared for me to join the team.

The assistant deanship proved for me an effective on-ramp into college administration. Dean Gates had structured the position as a sort of administrative internship which provided a reduced teaching load but kept me in the classroom while assigning me administrative roles that could address college needs and priorities. Some of my new functions, such as chairing the college curriculum committee, felt more like a simple shifting of seats in an area where I had already become immersed. There I found myself in a position where I could finally address some of the features of service in that area that had long annoyed me, such as overly lengthy meetings driven by excessive attention to minutia. Other duties, such as my charge to create and lead a new committee to oversee our homeless interdisciplinary programs, gave me the opportunity to develop new collegial relationships with a group of faculty from across the college and forge the group into a creative, productive team. We were able to rework many of the old area studies minors into attractive new programs that could be folded into a new interdisciplinary cultural competency major, develop a new graduate program in Cultural Resource Management, and put into place a meaningful annual program assessment of our interdisciplinary programs for the very first time. I remain proud of the successes we achieved, I still recall fondly the friendships I was able to develop, and the insight I gained into other disciplinary perspectives has served me well in my career to this day.

Eight months into my assistant deanship, my associate dean Rick Kurtz announced that he was leaving to take a deanship at nearby Ferris State University. Rick had become a good friend and I had looked forward to another year of working with him, but his departure confronted me with a new decision when Dean Gates asked me to serve as her interim associate dean for the next year. She invited me to consider applying for the permanent position, but she assured me that she could afford to wait on that and allow me to take my time considering that possibility while serving out the year's term in my interim capacity.

My year as an interim associate dean immersed me into the life of a college administrator while providing ample time to consider whether to pursue this path as a career. Friends and family outside of academia congratulated me on my "promotion." I accepted their good wishes with the explanation that this really represented more a change of direction, and one that I was still considering. The new duties I assumed included primary responsibility for faculty hiring and development, which reinforced my experience of college-level administration as a deeply communal enterprise in many ways. My duties engaged me in many stimulating conversations with department chairs along with candidates for hire and pre-tenure faculty. I joined the dean in her welcome dinners for newly hired faculty, gaining a chance to learn a little more about them on a personal level. I often joked that my interviews and pre-tenure conferences satisfied my appetite for dilettantism, since I could learn a bit about current trends in nearly every discipline represented in the college and ask follow-up questions about the fascinating research findings of those engaged and creative young scholars. I enjoyed playing a small part in their mentoring toward tenure and promotion and eventually enjoyed the privilege of celebrating with several I had advised who eventually grabbed that brass ring.

A similar sense of communal purpose attended most of my duties as associate dean, including many of the miscellaneous tasks that fell to me when the dean did not have time to do them. To be sure, many of them were simple one-and-done affairs, but they frequently served a human end—making classrooms a little more comfortable for teaching and learning or ensuring that colleagues had the environment and resources they needed to consult with students or pursue their research. Even my task of chairing the college grade grievance committee proved surprisingly rewarding as I led that group of colleagues in a process of deliberation over often thorny matters of student performance and evaluation. My own unfair opinions about some of my colleagues melted away as I watched the consideration they extended to both the dissatisfied students and the chagrined faculty members, the care with which they evaluated the evidence of the cases before them, and their commitment both to fairness and to academic integrity. I never concluded one of those sessions with the sense that either party had not been fairly heard or that the outcome was summarily rendered. I rarely felt—and still almost never feel—that administrative work was impersonal, boring, or soulless.

I spent most of that year as interim associate dean deliberating whether to remain in the role. I was pursuing a book project at the time and Dean Gates allowed me to block off weekly time for it, but the job did slow my progress exponentially. I kept a foot in the classroom by teaching one evening graduate course that fall semester, but I missed working with undergraduate students more closely. I discussed my options with my wife at home, with colleagues in my department, and with several different administrators in various university offices. The decisive conversation, however, took place in a car outside a local brew pub with a friend who had served two terms as a state legislator and who was at the time serving a gubernatorial appointment to a state agency. I told him my misgivings about leaving the faculty ranks to "join the Dark Side," particularly in view of those cases I had known of persons who chose the role primarily out of ambition for higher salaries and greater influence. He responded, "yes, but university administration needs good people too." His confidence in me as one of the "good people," a confidence shared by my own dean and the many colleagues who encouraged me, led me to throw my hat in the ring when the permanent associate deanship was announced. A search committee of university faculty selected me as their nominee to the dean, who appointed me to the post beginning with the 2013-2014 academic year.

Dean Gates also sent me to the Harvard Institute for Management Leadership in Education in June of 2014. That two-week experience cemented my commitment to higher education administration as I rubbed shoulders with academicians from across the country, engaged in lively and stimulating discussion with colleagues in the study group to which I was assigned, and learned from a succession of distinguished leaders. The first week's morning sessions consisted of an interactive and deeply personal exploration of Dr. Robert Kagan's recently-published *Immunity to Change* led by Kagan himself. Kate Conley, recently appointed dean of the faculty of arts and sciences at William & Mary, was my conversation partner during those sessions and proved a very empathetic listener, perceptive questioner, and deeply insightful observer. She helped me recognize that I could serve most effectively by relinquishing my remaining reservations and committing fully to my new role for however long the appointment might last. I returned to Central Michigan University ready to assume my new role without further reservation.

My years as associate dean at CMU continued to provide the interest and purpose I had experienced first as department chair and then as assistant and interim associate. A series of circumstances soon led Dean Gates to appoint me to the helm of her newly created School of Public service and Global Citizenship, in addition to my other duties. There I discovered a knack for building administrative structures within the college that could lend better order and efficiency to our programs and serve both faculty and students with fresh opportunities for education, collaboration, and service. I also gained literal construction management experience as college liaison to a major renovation of our flagship building, helping to coordinate the planning and preparation for the project and participating in multiple construction management meetings each week over an eighteen-month period. I could not have asked for a richer apprenticeship in the work of a college dean's office.

CMU also began encountering strengthening headwinds as I stepped into the associate deanship. In Fall 2011, the university had welcomed the largest freshman class in its history, but a scant two years later, dropping high school graduation rates across the upper Midwest cut into our enrollments and began creating a growing drag on our tuition-heavy budgets. The story was the same across Michigan's fifteen public universities: we were competing for the same shrinking pool of students. CMU's budget had suffered repeated blows throughout the volatility of the previous decade, which had hit Michigan even earlier than the rest of the United States, but this was different—steady declines projected over several years, not because of economic downturn and its impact on the state budget, but because of a major demographic shift (and here we are again!). The resulting budget pressures ultimately ended up undoing some of the projects I had developed, including the School of Public Service and Global Citizenship, which had to be eliminated three years after my departure. The experience taught me both the importance of understanding the budget and also the tremendous value of having a good budget analyst who could help us evaluate our diminishing resources against our strategic priorities and make the best strategic use of all available funds. The budget reductions curtailed our ambitions and led us to shelve projects we had planned. They also baptized me into one of the most painful of administrative tasks: personnel reductions. The union requirement to proceed by seniority made the process fairly straightforward, but it was a sorry business to have to notify good, hardworking instructors that their services were no longer needed.

Despite the difficulties of budget reductions with their attendant challenges, I became increasingly at home in the associate dean's office. I was able to establish a regular rhythm of work, my support staff was congenial and effective, and Dean Gates forged us into an effective, unified team who enjoyed working together in our efforts to make the College of Social and Behavioral Sciences into a place where faculty could thrive in their roles and where students could receive the best education we were capable of providing. I also found that my relationships with my faculty remained strong. Rarely did my position engender tension with colleagues in my department or elsewhere in the college. To the contrary, I was able to build more friendships not only across the college, but the wider university. I learned how to build and maintain the professional boundaries that discouraged my colleagues from attempting to trade on friendship for favors or special consideration. I also learned to reach out to my counterparts in other colleges across the university, most of whom had been in the roles longer and who were happy to share experiences and ideas that could help me do my job better.

Altogether, I spent five years in the dean's office of CMU's college of Humanities and Social and Behavioral Sciences, four of those years as associate dean. I enjoyed the work and learned to do it well—well enough, in fact, that by the fourth year as associate I began to wonder what might be next. I noticed that rarely did associate deans retire from the role: they either returned to faculty after a few years or went on to become a dean. I began to think that a deanship might actually lie in my future and decided to send out applications during the 2015-2016 academic year. My application attracted significant interest and landed me several initial interviews, but Samford University's Howard College of Arts and Sciences turned out to be the right fit for me. I had always thought that I would welcome the opportunity to work at a faith-based institution and I was met with encouragement at every point in the process. I left my final interview with President Andrew Westmoreland with the strongest sense of calling to a role that I have ever experienced. Confirmation came only three days later when Provost Michael Hardin called to offer me the deanship.

I am now in my sixth year as dean of Howard College of Arts and Sciences. That initial sense of vocation has not diminished, even though I have weathered my share of trials and challenges. Indeed, from the first week I set foot on campus, I found that my previous experience might almost have been tailored to fit this role, beginning with the $100,000 cut to my budget that greeted me on the way in the door, followed closely by the news that serious structural shortcomings in the university's program assessment were threatening to derail our upcoming accreditation review. In both instances, I had learned from training and experience what to do. I met the budget challenge with the able help of my administrative assistant, who found ways to reduce expenses with minimal harm to our recruiting and our strategic priorities.

The greater challenge of my first year by far was that of devising a program for college-wide assessment almost from scratch. Here I was able to tap experience in program assessment which I had begun to acquire during my earliest years as a junior faculty member at CMU and had developed to the point that, by 2010 I was tapped to lead the assessment team in preparation for that year's Teacher Education Accreditation Council (TEAC) accreditation review of the university's College of Education. I knew, however, that I could not single-handedly create a program of assessment on the scale needed without knowledgeable assistance. Early discussions of assessment among my department chairs at Samford called to mind similar misunderstandings of and objections to assessment that I had encountered at CMU almost two decades earlier. But during my second chairs' meeting, Don Bradley, the chair of Sociology at that time, picked up the conversation immediately to talk about backward design, how to distinguish between outputs and outcomes, how to align outcomes with effective assignments, and how to use findings to improve programs. I quickly appointed Don, who had previously served as an associate dean for planning and assessment in his college at East Carolina University, to serve as interim director for college assessment and appointed him associate dean the following summer. By October of 2017, he had led the college's program directors and department chairs in designing departmental assessment plans and collecting the first set of results and had made my college's assessment program a model for the entire university.

I could recount a major challenge for each year I have been dean of Howard College of Arts and Sciences. These would include the development and ongoing implementation of a college strategic plan, major renovation of three of our college's buildings, relocation of the great majority of our faculty to a single area of the campus, consolidation of several departments, and replacement of ten of the thirteen department chairs in the college. Each effort has required fresh efforts in creative thinking, problem-solving, negotiation, collaboration, and compromise. None of my actions have been universally accepted, but I have sensed solid faculty support throughout the process and enjoy a college leadership team that is capable and unified. I believe that the very core of my job is to find the best faculty and departmental leaders and to give them the equipment and resources they need to do their work well. I also believe deeply that clarity and transparency in both communication and processes are critical for effective leadership, faculty achievement, and college morale. My goal is to hire a generation of colleagues who are smarter than I am, to support them as best I can, and to get out of their way as much as I can.

I never anticipated when accepting this job that I would spend my fifth year leading through the greatest challenge of my generation's life. In early March 2020, I was enjoying a spring break breakfast with my wife and son when the provost called to inform me that Samford would be implementing the continuity of instruction plan the deans and chairs had been developing during the first half of the semester, shifting instruction entirely online for the remainder of the spring. The rest of that week and the beginning of the following became a blur of phone calls, online meetings, and email correspondence as we raced to put our plans into place. Many of our faculty members were taking up online teaching for the very first time, and much of the remainder of the semester was occupied with helping them to adapt to their environment, learn how to use our Canvas learning management system, and structure effective learning experiences for their students using unfamiliar tools and methodologies. A glance back at my April Outlook calendar reveals at least two chairs' meetings and three deans' meetings per week devoted to such matters as identifying and addressing problems of instruction, making on-the-fly adjustments in procedures, adjusting grading protocols, developing a one-time pass-fail policy, and conducting regular check-ins with one another on how we were coping and how we could help. I now have a hierarchy of email folders devoted entirely to managing the college's affairs during the pandemic.

As soon as the faculty had submitted their final grades, Samford's provost initiated development of a comprehensive plan for delivery of fall semester courses. He began by forming a Continuity of Instruction Task Force that drew upon Centers for Disease Control and Prevention (CDC), state, and county health guidelines to create a framework for planning that defined four scenarios corresponding to various levels of COVID-19 threat and adapting instruction to each. My associate deans and I then used that framework to plan for socially-distanced hybrid instruction across all programs. We also developed remote teaching accommodations for those faculty members with significant health risks. The planning process kept the dean's office busy full-time the entire summer and occupied the lion's share of the chairs' summer months as well. Meanwhile, Facilities Management prepared classrooms and a university

Pandemic Response Team developed procedures for robust testing, quarantining of those exposed, and isolation of students infected with COVID-19. By the time students returned to campus, we felt quite confident in the thoroughness of our plans but had little confidence that we would remain on campus the entire semester. The news of failures at other institutions such as the University of North Carolina at Chapel Hill suggested that we might not make it past the two week mark.

Despite our concerns, the Samford community remained on campus throughout the 2020-2021 academic year and exhausted faculty members and dragged their way across the finish line at the end of April 2021. Comprehensive planning, robust testing, masking, social distancing, and hand-washing did their work. We experienced a couple of worrying spikes during the fall semester in particular, but prompt action prevented an outbreak. Our Pandemic Response Team tracked patterns of infection and exposure and made adjustments between fall and spring semesters. Frequent campus-wide testing and constant attention to data, government outlets, and statewide trends permitted the team to fine-tune our monitoring and response. In contrast to general trends in Alabama, most faculty and a large majority of students took advantage of the vaccines as soon as they became available. By August, 2021, Samford's faculty were already vaccinated at a rate of 91%, while the student rate approached 70% and has since topped that. Samford University is now fully face-to-face, albeit masked in the classrooms, and the weekly rate of student COVID-19 infections has remained 15 or fewer throughout the semester.

The higher education community will be spending years compiling and analyzing the lessons learned from this period. Crucial elements of teaching, learning, and management will change forever. For me, however, some of the most important lessons remain human and relational. One important aspect of leading during this very uncertain time has been to maintain a sense of community, however diminished, among the faculty and students. My weekly messages to the faculty by either video or email received many expressions of appreciation. My entire leadership team responded conscientiously to every email to address problems and concerns and find resources to help. Many faculty have told us that they feel the dean's office has supported them well. The faculty who taught remotely formed support groups by Zoom on which they encouraged each other, shared ideas, and socialized. During the winter break, we held a pair of online listening sessions with our faculty where they could debrief the semester's experience and exchange tips for teaching more effectively and taking care of themselves and each other. Out of those sessions we developed a spring plan for more frequent opportunities for online meeting and exchange to strengthen the faculty sense of connection and community with one another.

In the first book of J.R.R. Tolkien's *Lord of the Rings*, the wizard Gandalf converses with the hobbit Frodo about the rising Shadow that is about to engulf them all in the great war of their age. "I wish it need not have happened in my time," Frodo says. Gandalf responds, "so do I, and so do all who live to see such times. But that is not for them to decide. All we have to decide is what to do with the time that is given us."[1] This pandemic has confronted all of us with an environment of uncertainty and flux that have challenged us with a constant flow of decisions that tax our creativity and resolve. I think that, on balance, I have made the right ones in my role as Dean of Howard College of Arts and Sciences. The disposition of my faculty, the confidence of my team, and the support of my provost suggest as much. I also take comfort from the sense of calling that has remained with me ever since I walked out of President Westmoreland's office almost five years ago. Ed Bastian, CEO (Chief Executive Officer) of Delta Airlines, observed at the beginning of the pandemic, after his company's revenues had dropped 95% in one month, that adversity can be our greatest opportunity. He said that it was an honor and a privilege to be managing at a time like this. It is our time.

Notes

[1] J.R.R. Tolkien, *Fellowship of the Ring* (New York: Ballantine Books, 1965), 82.

Five

Reinventing my "Why?":
A Journey of Discovery Through Deaning"

Valerio Ferme

University of Cincinnati

Abstract

Using the *topos* of the journey, the essay explores the trajectory that has taken me from faculty and chair of my department, via the subsequent stages of divisional dean for the arts and humanities at the University of Colorado, then dean of the College of Arts and Letters at Northern Arizona University and of the College of Arts and Sciences at the University of Cincinnati, to my current position as provost at the latter institution. At the core of this journey has been a desire to discover (and in some ways rediscover) what motivates me as an educator for whom the humanities and humanistic pursuits continue to matter. Significantly, my humanities background helped ground my response to the COVID-19 pandemic via the topos of storytelling and empathetic sharing. The article is a mix of biography and sharing of strategy and post-event reflections that loosely provides a bird's eye view into why someone might wish to undertake administrative career moves in higher education.

Keywords: Black Death, Giovanni Boccaccio, budget, Albert Camus, chair, companionship, COVID-19, data analysis, dean team, *The Decameron*, deficit, equity, fundraising, Italian Studies, journey, leadership, liberal arts, Martin Springer Institute, mentoring, Northern Arizona University, pandemic, path of self-discovery, *The Plague*, provost, public humanities, Santa Clara University, service, team, tenure-track faculty, University of Cincinnati, University of Colorado

***

I share the story of how I became a dean, hoping it might resonate with others. Early in my career, I developed an interest in leadership and took multiple service assignments to understand the inner workings of my department and college. I eventually became chair of my unit and then divisional dean at the University of Colorado, before being hired as dean of the College of Arts and

Letters at Northern Arizona University and eventually taking the position of dean of the college of arts and sciences at the University of Cincinnati (since writing this article, I have been appointed as provost of the university).

When I entered academia, I knew little of what deans do, except that service, the oft-maligned third wheel of a faculty's workload, is their mainstay. It soon would become mine as well. Indeed, service activities filled my early years as an assistant professor in a department of French and Italian, because I was the only active representative of the Italian faculty. Our bylaws required representation from both areas in departmental committees, and I was the default choice for Italian faculty. For me, becoming involved in departmental committees was a blessing: I learned more about the workings of the department, and it kept me on task to be productive with my time elsewhere. It also started me on the path of self-discovery that would inform my steps up the academic ladder to my current position.

The Journey Begins

In 2007, my senior colleagues asked me to consider becoming chair of the department, though I was still an associate professor. I accepted enthusiastically, spurred by the unanimous favorable vote (I ran unopposed)! Becoming chair appealed to me because it was my turn, as the next tenured faculty in line; I would be the department's first Italian chair after 20 years of French leadership; and, I had become the single-parent of two older adopted boys, so the extra pay came in handy, and the term was only three-years long. In 2010, I was re-elected to a second term; and, in 2014, to a third one, after a two-year hiatus following a leave of absence and a sabbatical. Interestingly, as I was finishing my first term as chair, the position of associate dean for the arts & humanities came open. Though I had not considered the role until then, favorable comments from fellow chairs alerted me that I might be dean material. In addition, the position intrigued me because I yearned to work collaboratively across disciplines to produce change, a characteristic that, by now, I felt was essential for my growth and that of the arts and humanities division.

My status as an associate professor held me back, though I felt I had the chutzpah to occupy the position. Five years later, when the then-divisional dean vacated the position, I applied. The years of waiting matured me. They also involved a change of scenery, when I took a leave from the University of Colorado to hold an endowed chair position at Santa Clara University with oversight over a multi-million dollar fund to promote Italian Studies. This position required me to create new programming for students while organizing conferences and cultural symposia. Always an introvert, the job challenged me to be on the go, call people, and meet functionaries, like the Italian consul, the mayor of San Francisco and second-tier celebrities. It shored up my confidence in handling large budgets, facilitating connections, and solving complex challenges. More importantly, I realized that I become more engaged when I advocate on behalf of ideas that matter to me professionally and personally, as when I organized a four-university tour for Italian filmmakers who documented the plight of African immigrants to Italy at the height of the Mediterranean crossings early in the twenty-first century. Though I left the position to return to Colorado, the experience as a connector between people and as a catalyst for new collaborations was valuable for how I perceive the dean role: someone motivated to act in the interest of others, who is intrigued by puzzles that require solving even when the pieces are not all visible, and who brings those pieces together to create new and successful wholes.

I returned to the University of Colorado in 2013. After a sabbatical semester during which I wrote most of my third book and completed a co-edited volume, I went back to my regular duties for a semester; submitted my promotion to full professor file; and was asked, once more, to be the chair of the department. Though less enthusiastic about resuming the role, I felt eager to apply my newly found outward-facing voice to the role. Serendipitously, as I began my third term, the dean announced that the divisional dean for arts and humanities was stepping down. Buoyed by my impending promotion, I submitted my application for the newly opened position. My two adopted sons were now officially adults. I was in a stable relationship after years of single parenthood. And I was ready to become a spokesperson for the arts and humanities.

If there ever is an ideal time for something to happen, this was it for me. I wanted to revamp my career. Publishing books and articles was still an exciting challenge, but I had completed three major projects in three years and had temporarily exhausted my energy for research. Teaching still brought the adrenaline rush of excitement, and the fundamental goal of helping young people find their voices remains a draw of an academic career (I still occasionally teach to understand student goals and expectations). Yet, leadership questions invited me to seek greater challenges: What makes a good administrator? How do we motivate individuals? What goals drive teams? In the twenty-first century, shared governance often clashes with the administrative desire for agility and quick response, so what is the best way to handle the conflicting demands of faculty and the upper administration? The final push, if I needed one, was provided by the pervasive public litany about the worthlessness of degrees in the liberal arts, and especially the arts and humanities, which took a more pernicious tone when President Obama, a liberal arts trained politician, publicly criticized the value of the liberal arts in a widely quoted pronouncement.[1]

I believed we were not doing enough in the arts and humanities to counter these negative arguments. My experience at Santa Clara taught me to shift from a reactive mode that claimed an intrinsic value that seemed obvious to us, to showing that value derived from the humanities could be applied to earning a living and living more productively. Emboldened by my previous foray into the field of public humanities and friend- and fund-raising for the liberal arts I had done at Santa Clara, I believed I was a good candidate.

That spring I was offered the job. I was elated. I reached out to my predecessor in the months before the transition, and we discussed every unit and his perspective on the chairs and directors of departments and programs. Though, as a current and former chair, I knew many of my colleagues well, I realized that interactions with peers change when you assume a position that leads them. Indeed, once I became the divisional dean for the arts and humanities, relationships that had been governed by amicable respect were transformed by the changed balance of our relationship. A handful of my fellow chairs distinguished the professional from the personal, and to them I am grateful for having provided insights and support through the challenges of my initial foray into deanship.

I spent my first summer as divisional dean meeting the chairs and directors of my units and every other administrator whose work might even tangentially interact with mine. I asked to meet in their office, regardless of how close or faraway they were from me on campus, to understand who they were in the comfort of their own spaces. I have applied these modes of procuring knowledge every time I have moved into new leadership roles at Northern Arizona University and the University of Cincinnati, and I recommend them to anyone who moves into an administrative role. Getting to know the people you will interact with accelerates one's knowledge into the behind-the-scenes organizational and operational structure of the university.

Concurrently, and more challenging, I worked to understand the college's metrics and finances. Delving into the numbers and financials of the division and college (course-loads, course releases, sabbaticals, local and general funds, endowments) became my first year's obsession. Even as chair, I had used data to inform qualitative decisions. Knowing the college's numbers can make or break one's effectiveness as dean. I also maintain that if you are a humanist, colleagues are more likely to assume that you are not a numbers' person, particularly administrators whose background is in fields where numerical data informs most decisions or research. As an example, five months into my divisional dean position, I created a chart that showed the teaching loads, averages, and course distribution for each faculty member in my units, that also explained and ranked departmental averages for individual and unit student credit hours and courses. In turn, this allowed me to counter arguments for increased funding and positions with a conversation about how we distribute teaching loads unfairly among faculty and across departments and start deeper conversations about best practices in teaching and research. My fellow associate deans were so impressed that they asked to provide the modeling for their own units.

Numbers do not tell the full story. However, a further practical reason for understanding them is to know what is happening in the units, via their organizational and financial strengths and weaknesses. New deans should gather as much information as possible from their business manager and data analyst (the latter an essential role in a contemporary dean's office) early on; and be humble enough to ask questions. While initially the complexity of data and terminology is overwhelming, eventually the numbers become a source of qualitative as much as quantitative knowledge. Conversely, the dean should ensure that the college's business staff has expert knowledge: good business analysts are worth their weight in gold. Know how your general and local funds work and how they can be used to support different missions, whether in a centralized system or in a responsibility centered management (RCM) model. Informed financial oversight becomes a life-saving measure in times of crisis, because knowing where there are pockets of money that can be used interchangeably can save a college dean from financial shortfalls.

Setting Out Over Uncharted Waters

I went on the market in the Fall of 2016, one year into my term as divisional dean. Going on the market is a learning experience. Uprooting oneself after decades in a place one calls home is painful, and forces one into a web of secrecy, as the conventional wisdom is that we do not want our boss to know we are seeking new opportunities. Going on the market required rethinking my career as I would be leaving an established reputation, colleagues that trusted and valued me, and, personally, a location and university considered among the most desirable in the country. Conversely, what kept me interested were the knowledge that, once before (at Santa Clara), I had been hired at an equally desirable university; and that, at this stage of my career, occupying administrative jobs had become *the thing that kept me engaged* as I grew personally and professionally. Indeed, the support I received internally from members of our dean team gave me the confidence to accede to the next administrative level and try my hand at transforming it.

Entering the recruiting arena offered a new perspective on the academy and its internal pecking order. I learned that recruiters often determine where you might be a good fit by the university where you work.[2] Jobs at the most prestigious universities are often off-limits to those who do not come from similarly ranked universities. Also, I realized that the ideal job will not come into view immediately. I wanted to become a dean at a college of arts and sciences at a large public, research-one university (R-1), but typically I was being considered for jobs as dean of arts and letters at smaller institutions.

Though my ego was hurt, my philosophy has always been to show that, once given a job, I can exceed its boundaries. So, in the spring of 2017, I was offered the job of dean of the College of Arts and Letters (CAL) at Northern Arizona University (NAU).

This job was not on my radar when I entered the market, and yet it checked a number of boxes. The university has grown its research enterprise substantially in recent years, in line with its enrollment growth, to pursue research-one status. It also was growing at a time when many universities were not. Moreover, for someone for whom diversity and inclusion are important, it provided the unparalleled opportunity to collaborate with the greatest concentration of Native American nations in the country. And, because it is in an area of the country that I have long loved for its geological beauty and quasi-mythical western history, it suited my personal and emotional needs. Finally, not to be discounted, I developed an instant rapport with the then-provost, whose thoughtfulness during the interviewing process suggested a cooperative style I would welcome in the position.

Dean on a High Desert Island

Moving to Northern Arizona had challenges. CAL was among the smallest colleges at the university, with fewer majors than most. A strong general education core shored up its finances and faculty numbers, as we delivered the third-most student credit hours in the university. But it also soon became apparent that, while nominally the university had a traditional structure in which academic affairs reported through the provost, everything was top-down, through the office of the president.

I had looked forward to becoming a dean buoyed by the (mistaken) belief that I could control budgets and apportion them strategically to benefit quality growth via targeted initiatives. This was not true at NAU. Deans had little control of college moneys and all expenses were monitored. Even awarding tenure-track lines, replacing office staff and distributing temporary instructional monies to departments needed the president's rather than the provost's imprimatur. Within three months, the lack of financial responsibility became the least favorite part of the job.

In hindsight, I became dean at NAU naively thinking that, during the interview process, I had capably assessed the situation on the ground and asked the right questions. When offered the job, besides negotiating for a higher salary than I was making and a departmental right-to-retreat with a salary comparable to my Colorado one, my basic concerns had been to secure discretionary money for new initiatives; find out whether the college had a budget deficit; and decide if I should make personnel changes to my team. I had not asked the fundamental question of whether I could ensure the financial health of the college via internal and external shared processes. Not doing so diminished my agency tenfold; and, had I known how budgetary decisions flowed at the university, I might have reconsidered the offer. The experience served me well when I moved to Cincinnati because, before accepting my new position, I asked to see the college's budgets, requested additional discretionary moneys, interviewed extensively the associate deans and other members of the dean's team, and negotiated significant budget deficit reductions to shore up the college's financial position. The offering of a position is the point of highest leverage for a dean: institutions do not like to lose their top candidates, so that is the time when you can demand the most honesty and clarity, as well as budgetary concessions in the process.

I also soon realized that at NAU the upper administration viewed the College of Arts and Letters as a problem child, either because its faculty occupied leadership positions in the Faculty Senate, a body that often clashed with the president, or because we had retrenched to well-worn arguments that the college did not have adequate resources due to public discourse that continued to belittle its value for a twenty-first-century education. The redistribution of resources toward more practical, professional majors and hires in the years that preceded my arrival produced a general feeling that faculty and staff were undervalued, a not uncommon perception in the humanities and arts across the country, but more pronounced in a college that had seen its faculty slashed by as much as 20% in tenure ranks during the previous five years.

The difference between coming into the dean's role as an outsider to the institution is significant. At CU (University of Colorado), I knew the lay of the land. The outsider does not have that advantage, though many universities prefer national searches for executive positions because bringing in a fresh perspective gives everybody the opportunity to reframe processes, questions, and situations through different lenses. The greatest disadvantage an external dean faces is not knowing the players or the dynamics at play. It takes time to understand the people, internal relationships and administrative shortcuts that get the work done. As dean, I faced the sediment of privilege that some faculty and units in the college had enjoyed for years. For example, as soon as I applied my data-driven, equitable approach to teaching and student credit hours distributions to faculty and departments, I discovered that, though the standard teaching load per semester was three courses for TT (tenure-track) faculty, and four courses for adjunct faculty, the exceptions were so many and often unexplained that compliance with the requirements required college-wide conversations and was challenged each semester.

NAU sits in Flagstaff, on the edge of (but ostensibly on) Native American tribal lands, close to the high desert plains of the Grand Canyon, Four Corners, and

Navajo National Monument. Flagstaff's population has tripled in the past 20 years, mostly via the influx of wealthy Californians, and reverse-snowbirds who live in the Phoenix valley and purchase homes among the Ponderosa Pines to enjoy the milder summer temperatures of its 7,000ft. elevation. It became evident early in my tenure that the president wanted me to interact well with the new wealthy denizens of the city. Because CAL holds the School of Art and a well-known School of Music, as well as a renowned center for the study of the Holocaust and interfaith dialogues (the Martin Springer Institute), it is the most outward-looking college within the university. This geo-cultural and economic reality became the leverage to escape the budgetary constraints of the university's top-down model of governance.

To succeed I pursued a two-pronged attack. On the one hand, I engaged our office of development to establish strong connections not only with donors in Flagstaff and the Phoenix area, but also with city cultural leaders—citizens and organizations—with whom the college interacted for much of the artistic and cultural engagement they so desired. In two years as dean, CAL achieved two of the three highest fundraising years in its history, highlighted by the completion of a new Recital Hall which, begun prior to my arrival, became one of the president's most important achievements. On the other hand, and more rewarding for wanting to make a difference in this role, I focused on promoting educational and cultural relationships with Native American nations; and emphasized the specific bent of a college faculty well-known for its activism and community engagement, with many leaders in the areas of sustainability, the environment, and the relationship of the university with Native American people.

I was hired to raise the college's research profile and to create transparency in its policies. In two years, using data and comparing documents on teaching and research loads, we revamped promotion and tenure requirements; created mentoring documents; tightened loopholes in sabbatical leaves; and created greater accountability in the evaluation of the performance of faculty and staff. We achieved these changes by involving faculty and chairs of each department and by communicating consistently throughout the implementation process. What ultimately proved most difficult for me to accept were the unpredictable budgetary cuts and the constant sense of impending crisis that, after the first year, enveloped the university. Having failed as a university to meet our enrollment target growth, I spent my days bogged down in the minutia of crisis mode, managing faculty shortages and plugging budgetary holes. Though rewarding because our ability to move fungible funds and cooperate with the units enabled us to face these crises, the lack of agency became too much to handle on an ongoing basis.

Pushing Off Again

My years at NAU were invaluable. However, my work environment was not ideal. The school experienced high attrition at all levels of leadership, highlighted by my serving under three provosts in two years. I soon was ready for a bigger role, with a clear focus on landing a position as dean of a college of arts *and sciences* at a research-one university.

My second go-round on the job market attracted more inquiries and interest from recruiters. Initially, I almost overlooked the announcement of a dean search by the college of arts and sciences (A&S) at the University of Cincinnati (UC). Once I researched the university's role as a civic institution in service of the city and its focus on experiential learning via one of the largest co-op programs in the nation, I changed my mind. The interview revealed a messy situation, with the faculty strongly aligned with the previous dean and the administration struggling with the deficit it imposed upon the college via a RCM-model that created both a multi-million-dollar revenue hole and a $5M expense deficit mark. Eventually, I was offered the job and, after requesting substantial budgetary support via the negotiations I described earlier in the essay, I took the job.

I grew immensely through the challenges of these two years. For one, with the help of my dean's team and heads, we managed to close the revenue deficit, and achieve significant revenue surplus that we were able to 'reinvest' when the university dictated an 8% across-the-board cut in permanent funding from all the university units. In addition, our data-driven approach to financial management, and the close collaboration between the dean's financial office and the departments allowed us to reduce A&S's expense deficit from $5M to $800K, results no one expected in the midst of the current challenges. While we have hired, we have done so judiciously, balancing needs in high enrollment areas with the desire to increase our diversity (35% of our tenure-track hires have been minorities). Prior to the pandemic, 2020 had turned out to be an unqualified success. In addition, the college broke its one-year fundraising record by topping the $13M mark. More importantly, we created a solid strategic plan that aligned our efforts with the president's strategic initiative of Next Lives Here.[3]

COVID-19: Into Unknown Waters

For everyone in academia, the pandemic has been all-consuming for the past two years. The immediate consequences were the deserting of campuses with consequent loss of revenue; and the pivoting quickly to remote and online learning, with substantial costs to upgrade connectivity and computer capacity, and invest in training. The more durable aftermath has been the shifting directives colleges are issuing with regard to distancing, masking, testing and vaccination requirements, as strands of the virus force us into varied responses that run afoul, alternatively, of students, faculty, staff and the public. Moreover, we have all had to adapt to a new normal, which also includes figuring out how to ensure our financial viability, as presidents and CFOs announced and continue to announce cuts and retrenchments, as well as new investments in technology and recruiting strategies.

In 2020, COVID-19 scrambled the interval between the spring and fall semesters. Everyone who was a dean during the Summer of 2020 knows that the experience was like no other on three different fronts. For one, expected budgetary reductions involved constant revisions, based on drops in state funding, student enrollments and university functionality. This in turn forced deans to consider staff cuts, reductions in permanent positions, and cost-cutting measures that ranged from reducing graduate and adjunct budgets to instituting furloughs. On the enrollment side, our recruitment and advising groups had targets to 'land' the class, which required constantly cajoling admitted students to enroll and conversations with returning ones about the financial impact of COVID-19 on their return plans. As dean, I held town halls with parents during the confirmation process and then during the official advising and enrollment times, while monitoring and responding to data analytics streams that either dropped or lifted our advising unit's spirits week after week. Finally, on the academic side, it meant planning both a return of research to campus after a two-month shutdown, and a long-term shift from mainly face-to-face to mostly online and hybrid courses, with the proviso that everyone be ready to switch instantly to full-online delivery should infections in the fall surpass certain thresholds.

As intense as this was, the greatest challenge has been to communicate and uplift people's spirits during a crisis that extends into the current academic year (2021-2022). With everyone forced into distant communication, often occupying personal spaces, deans became conveners rather than authorities (and I feel the same in my current role as Provost). My humanities background helped. In my research, I studied another great health crisis in human history, the Black Plague of 1348, via Giovanni Boccaccio's *Decameron*.[4] Having written a monograph on this book, I found it (as well as Albert Camus' *The Plague*) helpful in responding to the pandemic.[5] In the prologue, Boccaccio states that, during the plague, Florentine authorities let the city descend into chaos (a claim I refute, as the city's government swiftly replaced its members when they succumbed to the plague and quickly implemented sanitary responses to stem the propagation of the disease). Boccaccio also sorted responses to the plague by the civilian population into four categories: those who retreated into their homes and shut off the world; those who continued as if nothing had happened;

those who, thinking the end was nigh, overindulged in the pleasures of the flesh; and those who tried to escape the areas of contagion. Boccaccio then shows the importance that storytelling plays in providing solace and respite as a mental palliative that brings comfort and laughter. On the other end of the spectrum is Dr. Bernard Rieux of Camus' *The Plague*, a disillusioned doctor who gives voice to the existentialist tenet of a life devoid of hope and who, nonetheless, shows compassion for the plague's victims because of the humanity they share and because his duty is to relieve human suffering.

As dean, I realized immediately that we needed to provide as secure a place as possible for our personnel's feelings of displacement and fear, even as we continued to project an aura of assuredness in navigating the confusion surrounding our financial and educational viability as institutions. Like Boccaccio's narrators in the *Decameron*, I made companionship and shared experiences the focus of my messages to bridge the distancing between our new spaces of operation and concurrent feelings of alienation and resentment. In evaluating my own emotions, I developed an empathetic response that communicates my own sense of loss, damage and fear to countless employees, faculty members and students who experienced and continue to experience the loss of companionship and socialization that our now-limited direct, face-to-face interactions support. Finally, I had to emote these experiences in public fora, as part of a shared, collective distress, that acknowledges our vulnerability, even as we make progress toward a new normal clouded by the uncertainty of a solution in the future.

The future into which we are emerging is unclear. Universities are now different from the havens of learning we knew in our own studies, or even in earlier incarnations of our administrative selves. Yet, in the midst of the crisis, new hope is emerging in the social unrest that has rocked the country, and in the loss of certainties and absolutes that even we in academia often hold dear. The opportunity is there to transform who we are and how we do things. In response to what has happened these past two years, in 2021 I created a Twenty-First-Century Arts and Sciences Task Force whose mandate was a year-long exploration of our core values and aspirations, and how we intend to pursue them into the near and fairly distant future. Now, as provost, I am hopeful that what we discovered and how we responded will continue to transform the whole of the university's educational mission. Universities have adapted and changed over the past millennium. The pandemic has turned our operations upside down. Now it is up to us to turn ourselves inside out and discover and/or rediscover a new purpose for the twenty-first century.

Notes

[1] Scott Jaschik, "Obama vs. Art History," *Inside Higher Ed*, January 31, 2014. https:// www. insidehighered.com/news/2014/01/31/obama-becomes-latest-politician-criticize-liberal-arts-discipline.

[2] Jason Brennan and Phillip Magness, *Cracks in the Ivory Tower. The Moral Mess of Higher Education* (New York: Oxford University Press, 2019).

[3] See University of Cincinnati. 2020. https://www.uc.edu/about/strategic-direction.html.

[4] Giovanni Boccaccio, *The Decameron,* trans. Wayne Rebhorn (New York: W.W. Norton & Co., 2014).

[5] Albert Camus, *The Plague,* trans. Stuart Gilbert (New York: Vintage, 1991).

Leadership for Institutional Change

Six

Making the Transition from Faculty to Dean during Major Institutional Change

Claire Oberon Garcia

Colorado College

Abstract

Colorado College's problems with race were not unique to it: like many small liberal arts colleges, until recently our student body had been predominantly white and socially and financially privileged. The college did the same old things that other colleges and universities had been doing and suggesting since the nineties to show that it "valued diversity." But clearly they weren't effective. We needed institutional change. The declaration to be an antiracist institution was a bold first step to fundamental transformation.

In 2019, Colorado College, after a series of high-profile racist incidents, made a commitment to become an antiracist college in all aspects of its operations. An antiracist approach to diversity, equity and inclusion radically reorients how an institution deals with race and other minoritized categories on campus by shifting the focus firmly to structural and systemic inequities that are created by policies, procedures, practices and systems of accountability. It avoids the trap of debating whether or not certain thoughts, words, people or behavior can be rightfully characterized as racist and instead focuses on the *effects* on equity and inclusion of policies and practices and behavior. Part of the antiracist commitment involved a reassessment of its financial model, which is heavily dependent upon full-pay, mostly white and privileged students and rethinking how the liberal arts are relevant to the 21st century lived realities of our students. Add to the these challenges national racial unrest, a global pandemic, and abrupt changes in senior leadership, and one Black woman dean finds herself at the center of a college in the throes of an unprecedented and multifaceted time of institutional change.

Keywords: anti-Black, anti-discrimination policy, antiracist institution, antiracism plan, Black faculty, Chief Diversity Officer, Colorado College, COVID-19, DEI, diversity, equity, general education, Carolyn Hodges, institutional change, leadership, loneliness, liberal arts education, pandemic, people of color, procedures and policies, Race, Ethnicity, and Migration Program, racial strife, racism, racist, structural and system inequity, Titles VI, VII, and IX, *Truth Without Tears,* Olga Welch

***

When I was appointed dean of faculty, a new position that came into being when my college hired its first provost, Colorado College was already in the midst of what we considered at the time major institutional change. After an ever-escalating series of racist incidents, many of which targeted Black faculty, students, and staff, the college had undergone an external review of racism the year before I started my new position. Long marginalized in my own department and in college governance, I desired a leadership position but had finally accepted that if I wanted to advance my career, I would have to seek opportunities elsewhere. For over thirty years, the only Black person in a position of structural leadership at my college had been the same vice president for student life, and only two people of color had ever been in the president's cabinet.

When I started in the dean's office, I knew that I had challenges ahead. In the wake of the findings and recommendations of the external review, Colorado College leadership had made a commitment that the college would become an antiracist institution. The faculty was divided on this issue and many others; it was fractured and fractious. There were many divisions among the faculty along generational, divisional, and political lines. We were also set to implement radically revised general education requirements that required the creation and approval of many new courses. While many of my colleagues were supportive of my taking on the role, they acknowledged the unprecedented sense of crisis shared by many students, staff and faculty, and the particular challenges of being a woman in leadership at the time. Little did we know that about halfway through my first year in transition from faculty member to dean, the racial strife that had been percolating across the nation at an ever-increasing temperature since 2016 would explode worldwide, and that a global pandemic would disrupt not only spring semester but the fundamental structures and practices of college life for the foreseeable future.

Colorado College was well positioned on two of the fronts of the national crises of 2020: we had already embarked on a rigorous antiracism plan and our distinctive academic calendar, where students take one course at time for 3 ½ weeks, gave us greater flexibility when sending students home in the spring of 2020 and welcoming them back to campus that following fall. But when the president announced in January that she was leaving the college in June, and in June the provost, who was supposed to serve as interim president during the year of the search, left the college abruptly, I suddenly found myself in a senior leadership position, reporting directly to two interim co-presidents who had valiantly stepped up to the plate from their cabinet-level administrative positions with no more than 48 hours' notice. The title of this essay, which was originally a panel presentation at the January 2020 Modern Language Association conference, suddenly took on yet another dimension.

Antiracism

Colorado College's problems with race were not unique to it: like many small liberal arts colleges, until recently our student body had been predominantly white and socially and financially privileged. The college did the things that all colleges routinely do: created a multicultural center, had an office in student life devoted to addressing the needs of students who were categorized first as "minority and international" and then "students of color and international." Departments were encouraged to "value diversity" when doing tenure-track searches, and although a handbook from the dean's office gave suggestions about where to place ads to up the chances of getting a diverse pool of candidates, departments were still having conversations that assumed that a candidate who contributed to compositional diversity might not be "the most qualified candidate." We were doing the same old things that other colleges and universities had been doing and suggesting since the nineties to show that we "value diversity." But clearly, they weren't effective. We needed institutional change. The declaration to be an antiracist institution was a bold first step to fundamental transformation.

The "straw that broke the camel's back" and finally propelled us into new ways of thinking about our racial issues was a white supremacist email that was sent to hundreds of students, faculty and staff from an outside account. The email made reference to a controversial student conduct decision regarding students who had posted anti-Black remarks on social media, and insulted the only two Black administrators on campus. Similar emails, with details slightly changed, showed up at other colleges and universities that year. The college's first response was to tell those who had received the email to simply delete it: leadership did not at first realize the depth of the wounds that such an email caused, especially its vile attack on two well-respected and long-serving college leaders. Later official missives acknowledged the trauma the emails had caused in the community, but the college administrators' response was still deemed inadequate by Black people, Indigenous people and People of Color (BIPOC) students, faculty, and staff. BIPOC students met for hours with our then-president, in whom they found an attentive and empathetic listener. At the penultimate faculty meeting of the year, our president ceded the time usually spent for her report to the faculty to the Black Student Union. Their presentation to the assembled faculty started with a student's heartfelt poem about her experiences as a Black student at Colorado College; other students joined with their brief first-person testimonies. Then students called out particular individuals, programs, and departments for what the students saw as their repeat racist behavior that had continued without consequence. Most of the examples they gave had been described, though in anonymized form, in a recent campus climate survey. As my home department was "called out," along with specific colleagues, I felt a deep sense of shame along with pride at the students' desperate courage and empathy for my colleagues whose names were announced. The silence among the over 150 faculty present was the most profound I had ever experienced in a crowd. The faculty was shocked, but galvanized. Within minutes after the departure of the student group, the faculty voted by a wide margin to abolish the long-contested western civilization requirement. But what next?

The president assembled an advisory group to help organize an external review of racism at Colorado College. The college hired Dr. Roger Worthington, then director of the University of Maryland's Center for Diversity and Inclusion in Higher Education, to conduct the review. The advisory group chose this organization from a pool of proposals by several diversity consultant firms because it is a research center with a focus on higher education. Dr. Worthington was in residence at Colorado College for a month, sitting in on classes and student group meetings and meeting with various constituencies and units throughout the college. The result was an extensive report with a series of broad-ranging yet very specific recommendations. The board of trustees and president made an institutional commitment to become an antiracist institution.

An antiracist approach to diversity, equity and inclusion radically reorients how an institution deals with race and other minoritized categories on campus by shifting the focus firmly to structural and systemic inequities that are created by policies, procedures, practices and systems of accountability. It avoids the trap of debating whether or not certain thoughts, words, people or behavior can be rightfully characterized as "racist "and instead focuses on the *effects* of policies and practices and behavior. My college pledged to make the commitment to become antiracist and has started a thorough review of all policies and procedures in all units: one of the first documents to undergo this scrutiny was the student conduct handbook. The vice president and dean of student life hired an outside expert to revise the handbook in consultation with current students and staff. On the academic side, we started reviewing the hiring, review, and tenure and promotion procedures. Departments began reviewing their own curricula and major requirements through an antiracist lens. Human Resources pledged to root out racist policies and procedures in their office. All units and offices started the work, but much of it depended upon expertise from someone trained and experienced in diversity, equity, and inclusion (DEI) issues in higher education.

The external review had recommended that we hire a chief diversity officer (CDO). But for the kind of focused, in-the-trenches work we needed to do in the areas associated with staff, students, and faculty, it wasn't a job for one person. Too often a CDO's duties are described as "monitoring," "facilitating," "advising": words that don't suggest decision-making power to make change. I felt that we needed experts who were empowered and knowledgeable to produce change in these areas while collaborating for institutional transformation, and two civil rights lawyers who served on the board of trustees and I persuaded senior leadership that this was a better direction for Colorado College to go: it accorded more with our decentralized, collaborative and hands-on culture, and studies coming out of other colleges and universities seemed to suggest that targeted efforts were more meaningful than hiring one magical person to fix everything by sitting at the cabinet level and reporting to the president. But not many people agreed at first, arguing that a cabinet position in itself signaled authority and power. Once most people heard the rationale for hiring three people—one who would focus on staff development and business contracts; a teacher-scholar with DEI expertise who would focus on curricular, pedagogical and faculty career development from candidacy to emeritx; and someone who would focus on student issues and direct the campus multicultural center—most were convinced and excited that this was a way to create real change.

We spent the fall semester developing a job description for a senior associate dean for equity, inclusion and faculty development using ideas that emerged from focus groups, department chairs and program directors, and the Faculty Executive Committee. We had finalized all three job descriptions and just had our first meeting with the search firm consultant when, like everyone else, COVID-19 landed on U.S. shores and we told our students not to return after spring break. This decision had an immediate financial impact that included the loss of room and board revenue, and senior leadership decided that it was necessary to freeze all searches. Once again, I—this time joined by one of the other search committee chairs—found myself arguing for a course of action that deviated from expectations and seemed, to some, too risky. However, I was convinced that as we had described these positions as essential to the implementation of the antiracism goals that spoke to our core mission of providing the best liberal arts education in the country, to suddenly treat them as expendable and to put off moving forward on the antiracism front would tell the community that we were not really serious about the urgency of institutional change on the equity and inclusion front. We got a waiver to proceed with the hires and have them on board for the next academic year.

The hiring of the senior associate dean for equity, inclusion and faculty development was a big piece of our first year as an antiracist institution but not the only piece that I was engaged with during my first year as dean. BIPOC faculty and students had long been demanding that the college hold professors accountable for violations of our anti-discrimination policy as well as Titles VI, VII and IX. While I tried to take a developmental approach to adjudicating both the formal and informal cases, knowing that all of our faculty genuinely aspire to be good teachers to our increasingly diverse student body, I was working in an environment shaped by the perception—and too often the perception aligned with reality—that the college tolerated faculty behavior that should not be tolerated, and if faculty suffered any consequences for complaints supported by evidence, those consequences were "a slap on the wrist" that didn't accord with the seriousness of the confirmed violations. Like many new deans who have been hired internally, it was sometimes difficult to navigate seeing colleagues that I had liked and respected for years accused of behavior that was perceived to be disrespectful and/or discriminatory. Knowing that all of my colleagues want to be effective teachers, and honoring how important their identity as professors is to them, I have tried to take a developmental rather than a punitive approach to issues. Difficult conversations would sometimes end in hugs, with a whispered, "I hope HR doesn't see this." Luckily, I discovered in working with our Human Resources office that we share the same values and commitment to the college's mission and community, so in my first year we developed a relationship based on trust, support, and frank communication. In our second year, we worked on clarifying and communicating the procedures for investigations, especially in light of the changes to Title IX procedures. Most of our investigations now are conducted by external investigators.

But our first spring semester as an antiracist institution was turbulent. Communication between administration and the community at large was ineffective, as shown by the fact that a student list of demands that "rejected the antiracism plan in its entirety" included a demand to review the student conduct handbook: as I mentioned earlier, that spring, a special consultant and former post-doc fellow was conducting just such a review. I felt muzzled as a new member of administration: I was in the odd position of finding myself invisible, as when the student protesters repeatedly spoke of "an all-white administration," as well as silenced, as when I wanted to respond to the student protestors personally but was told that there had to be a "cabinet response." Although I was welcome to contribute to the cabinet response, that response took several days, at a time when I wanted to respond to the student petition within hours of receiving it. Later in the summer, as the world was convulsed by outrage over Breonna Taylor, Ahmaud Arbery, and George Floyd's murders, with our community dispersed, I felt yet another loss in not being able to have the discussions and protests that we would have had had we all been on campus.

Becoming an antiracist institution in a world shaped by the coronavirus threats and global response to exposures of the fundamental inequities in our society as well as the rise and legitimizing of white supremacy in the United States has become even more difficult than we imagined. But I firmly believe that a high-quality liberal arts education will equip our students well to confront the challenges ahead.

The Pandemic

As I write this at the start of Thanksgiving week in 2020, our college, county and nation are dealing with a horrifying surge in both cases and deaths due to the coronavirus. Our local hospitals are strained, and even as the Centers for Disease Control and other medical experts plead for Americans to forego traveling and gathering around tables with family members from multiple generations, millions of Americans are crowding airports and planes and declaring that getting together in a time of crisis is worth the risk to their elderly relatives and the general public. Whether or not our cultural predisposition to individualism and immediate gratification will lead to a collapse of our health care system and thousands more deaths, is a chapter in history that will have been written by the time you read this.

Colorado College, thanks to a rigorous randomized testing and contact tracing system and lessons learned when, at the beginning of fall semester, two of our largest dorms had to be quarantined, avoided outbreaks and had a far lower than expected incidence rate. An internal Scientific Advisory Group which consulted regularly with a consulting group of epidemiological and medical experts, and two COVID-19 safety and planning committees that represented all constituencies of the college, did amazing work in helping us make decisions that were informed by science and data. Navigating the logistical effects of the global pandemic—the adjustments to the academic calendar; the move to remote, hybrid and flex teaching formats, developing effective communication plan, etc.—was, of course, stressful and time consuming. But the hardest part of my job was supporting a faculty whose members, like everyone else, were profoundly emotionally affected by living through a pandemic.

Most faculty had concerns about their own and their loved ones' mental and physical health and wellbeing. Many faculty had major caregiving responsibilities, from children to elderly parents. Others were dealing with their own or family health issues, made more difficult by COVID-19 protocols. Everyone was adjusting to teaching in formats that most were unfamiliar with, and of course everyone—but especially pre-tenure people—were dealing with new feelings of inadequacy on the teaching and research fronts. I regularly consulted with chairs and directors for ideas about how best the college might support the emerging and often unprecedented needs of our faculty, and I sent out occasional messages reminding everyone to prioritize taking care of themselves, even at the expense of compromising their own standards of excellence. But most of the support that I was able to offer was on the individual level: regularly checking in with junior faculty as well as the many whom I knew were struggling; making sure that a conversation about self-care was touched on in every meeting; making myself available to those who might need a sounding board or practical help. While at first I felt compelled to keep up an image of calm, I soon learned that my colleagues appreciated knowing that I, too, had moments of struggle and an unprecedented work burden on top of the usual decanal responsibilities. Their consideration, support, and patience were essential to my being able to do my job through the crisis.

Liberal Arts for the Twenty-First Century

As a graduate of Bennington College with a double major in philosophy and creative writing, I had long described myself as someone with "a liberal arts approach to life" even before I re-entered academe as a professor. As a Black woman, though, I always had an uneasy relationship with academe, and was never at home in my predominately white department. As my teaching and scholarship was increasingly interdisciplinary and focused on both francophone and anglophone literature, I was told by my dean after a failed attempt to be promoted to the rank of full professor that my "department had no idea what I was doing" in my research and scholarship. I consistently got the message that my work and my experiences could not represent Colorado College faculty. While most post-tenure professors served at least a term on the Faculty Executive Committee (FEC), the faculty governing body, I was never elected. Three times I made it to a run-off: always against an older white man, one of whom had served five terms on the FEC. Three times I lost. I also ran for the divisional governing committee—the Humanities Executive Committee (HEC), but again, always lost, once in a run-off against a white male colleague many years my junior. After the election, which was held in real-time at a divisional meeting, a friend in another department approached me to explain why she had voted for the other candidate: "I thought that it was important that he have experience in governance," she said. At that point, I had been at the college for over twenty years and had never served in elected office.

A vocal advocate for DEI issues and director of our ethnic studies program, I realized that most of my colleagues did not see me as someone who could represent them. On the departmental level, I also realized that I would never chair my department—again, a very unusual position for a senior faculty member. When we held departmental retreats to draft the plan of succession for the next ten to twelve years, my name never came up, even as my departmental colleagues adjusted timelines to accommodate junior faculty's promotion and sabbaticals. I found an area in college life where I could make a difference in helping build the ethnic studies program and work with devoted fellow travelers to make it a major, one of the professional accomplishments that I am most proud of to this day. But even that project made me feel as if I were, in John Keats' words, "writing on water": the same semester that marked the Race, Ethnicity and Migration program's first year as a major, personality conflicts among the affiliated and core faculty imploded the program. Wanting the nascent program to be able to thrive and meet the needs of the enthusiastic students who were rushing to the new major, I resigned as director of the program. A call out of the blue from a headhunter made me realize for the first time that maybe the next stage of my career might be in administration, though not at my own institution. My first foray onto the job market in thirty years brought me to the semi-finalist position in one search, a finalist position in the one other that I applied to. I decided, with the support of the then-president, to put together a plan to make myself a competitive candidate for a program director or associate dean at another institution. I would "get my book out" and then, the following year, hit the job market again. It was only a series of flukes that resulted in my becoming dean of faculty at my own institution. I was such an outsider candidate for the position of dean of faculty at my own college that even in the confidential period when the provost had extended the offer but I hadn't accepted it, colleagues were telling me with confidence who the next dean would be: and it was always a name not my own. Like many small, highly selective liberal arts colleges, Colorado College had not only been predominately white, but was also in its histories and dominant ideologies, anti-Black. For many of my colleagues, a Black woman dean of Colorado College was probably unimaginable: though they were aware that I was in the running, it never occurred to them that I would get an offer.

For many of us, academe has never been an Ivory Tower, remote and protected from political and social strife. But in the past few years, the unraveling of civic norms, the power of social media, and the resurgence of violent expressions of white supremacy, anti-Blackness and misogyny have deeply affected our lives and relationships both within and outside of our classrooms on a daily basis. The increasing class and political polarizations that mark our national life are played out on campus. The vanishing middle-class and the intransigent racialization of class and educational opportunity are reflected in the shocking statistic that in the academic year 2019-20, 80% of my college's white students are paying full tuition, and 73% of BIPOC students were on need-based financial aid. The American education system, long-touted as an engine of social mobility, is now anything but. Instead, as studies by Georgetown's Center on Education and the Workforce and others have shown, colleges and universities play a major role in perpetuating the class divide and social inequality—conferring more advantage on those already possessing social and economic capital, and further disadvantaging those with few family and community resources.

Antagonism against Black, Indigenous, and People of Color is no longer covered up by racial etiquette in the world at large, and as the external review of racism and antiracism made clear, our on-campus racial etiquette is being stress-tested. Discussions about whether or not we can separate American democratic ideals and principles from American practice of white supremacy have taken on an existential urgency. If racism is indeed "baked in our DNA," as more and more people are saying, what hope is there that our politics and political leadership can reflect the gloriously various country that we in fact are? The Founding Fathers whose views prevailed were afraid of what a real democracy looks like, and the recognition of voting and other citizenship rights of those who were not white and male and straight have only been won through resistance, struggle, and sacrifice to state-sanctioned violence on the part of those excluded Americans.

All humanity faces an existential threat that respects neither race nor nationality, but it is the most vulnerable and poor that have been the first to suffer the effects of climate change. The problems of climate change are inextricably bound up with issues of power and equity on a global level. We must do more than we are doing now to address climate change, but our national leadership refuses to take action.

The world our students are entering to build lives, develop satisfying careers, and make a difference is complicated, marked by competing narratives and discursive and material strife and now, the ongoing effects of the coronavirus. In a nation shaped by "truthiness" and contempt for scientific and other forms of knowledge, how do we promote the value and efficacy of the long-touted liberal arts "critical thinking skills"?

Fifty years ago next year, the Colorado College faculty approved a radical new academic calendar: the block plan, where students would take and professors teach one class at a time, without periods or bells or set schedules. Their willingness to take such a huge risk was both a response to and a reflection of the upheaval of the times: the 1960s had also been a time of often violent and pervasive social and political conflict and change, and the decision to experiment with a new academic calendar was made with a sense of urgency as to what a liberal arts education should offer smart, curious young people in what felt like unprecedented times. The faculty had to invent something new, in a spirit of hope and risk when the world seemed to be falling apart at the seams and Colorado College's survival seemed far from assured.

Small, residential liberal arts colleges are at a similar moment of history today, both globally and in the United States. Human and other forms of life are threatened with extinction, yet powerful interests prevent us from managing the effects of climate change on a governmental level. Racism persists, in virulent forms that sadly seem to be reminiscent of days gone by. Our two-party democracy is being tested as what we thought were checks and balances and guardrails are proving inadequate against demagoguery. Higher education, both public and private, is subject to increasing scrutiny and distrust, while colleges and universities continue to play their part in increasing the privilege of those who are already privileged, and further limiting the prospects of those who are already at an economic and social disadvantage.

How can we best prepare our students—smart, curious, eager to make a difference in the world, often ambitious, often anxious—to understand what is going on? Through the liberal arts, which offers them the historical and cultural contexts for how we think/live in the present day, introductions to various disciplinary ways of thinking about and theorizing phenomena, and global perspectives. Colorado College is already great at consistently offering our students an engaging, meaningful curriculum, but this isn't the time for highly selective small liberal arts colleges (SLACs) such as ours to rest on our laurels. Most SLACs operate on a financial model that depends upon full-pay, predominantly white students rather than endowment revenue; given the coming "birth dearth" among white, affluent families and now the losses created by the coronavirus pandemic, it is not sustainable.

The time calls for us to build something new out of our considerable strengths as liberal arts colleges: we must approach the demands of making liberal arts education the best and most relevant form of education for the twenty-first century. The stakes are high. I'd love to recapture my own institution's experimental spirit by thinking even more boldly about what we offer our increasingly diverse students. I'd like to offer our students even more trans-, inter- and multidisciplinary experiences, where they can apply theories and methodologies from a variety of disciplines to complex and multifaceted questions, issues, and problems. I fantasize about offering even more classes and majors that offer integrative experiences built on a student's strong grasp of different disciplines' questions, theories, and methods, and administrative structures that reflect that integrative approach.

An environment supportive of experimentation and multi-, inter-, and transdisciplinary approaches to the big questions of our moment in history in a community of trust is exactly what a small liberal arts college can offer. This is another area where the dynamics on our campus reflect those of the larger society. A *sine qua non* of trust is transparency. Operating principles and policies must be created with buy-in from the constituencies they affect;

communicated clearly and consistently; and changed when they don't serve the needs of our students and key stakeholders. Trust among members of a community cannot be maintained without respect.

As dean of faculty, I try to do what I can from my position to foster a climate of trust and respect. This does not mean, though, that liberal arts faculty will not have awkward or even painful conversations, that rivalries will not exist between departments with bursting enrollments and those with dwindling enrollments, or that class and racial strife will not continue to shape relationships both in and outside of the classroom. But I have a deep faith in the traditional SLAC commitment to nurturing the intellectual and social growth of students and the power of knowledge.

Loneliness as Freedom

Like many BIPOC faculty, my relationship with my institution is complex and fraught. In my career of over 30 years at my college, I have had splendid opportunities and privileges but have also been deeply wounded, professionally and personally by bias and anti-Blackness. By the time that I made the transition from faculty to administration, I had learned several hard lessons that allowed me to approach the new position with equanimity and fortitude. My marginalized status over the years has allowed me to take on the position with an emotional detachment that would not have been possible even five years ago. My experiences with our ethnic studies program made clear to me that colleagues are not necessarily friends, and that fierce shared commitment to a common goal in the workplace does not necessarily create community. I am able to focus on my work in a way that is not dependent upon people knowing me or liking me, but judging me on how effective I am at my job.

One of the first books that I read upon my appointment was *Truth Without Tears: African American Women Deans Share Lessons in Leadership* by Carolyn R. Hodges and Olga M. Welch, the first Black women to serve as deans at their respective predominantly white institutions.[1] When I first read their book, I didn't understand a central tenet of their advice for successful leadership: to separate the role and responsibilities of being a dean from their personal selves, "Olga" and "Carolyn." They each listened, weighed evidence, evaluated arguments and made decisions as "dean." They developed strategies and plans as "dean." They related to colleagues and coworkers in their role as "dean." I thought that this approach would be difficult, even unhealthy. But after a few months in my position, I realized that this separation of "dean of faculty" and "Claire" is not only necessary to be an effective leader, but also for one's mental health and sense of self. To do my job effectively, I must have the trust of my colleagues that I make decisions that will ultimately benefit the academic mission of the college and our community; that I am committed to diversity, equity, and inclusion in all aspects of institutional life; and doing what I can from my position to create an environment where all faculty can thrive at all stages of their careers, yet be accountable to our institutional values.

In a recent article published in *Inside Higher Ed.*, Drs. Hodges and Welch reflected on higher education leadership during a global pandemic, and stated that "[m]oral courage must always trump inaction and silence":

> We believed then and now that to benefit those whom you serve and to lay the groundwork for long-term positive outcomes, moral courage trumps inaction and silence. Audre Lorde expressed it well in her poem "A Litany for Survival": "When we speak, we are afraid our words will not be heard or welcomed. But when we are silent, we are still afraid. So it is better to speak ..." Serving without fear will not ensure the permanence of your goals and plans. But only by maintaining the courage to speak inconvenient truths can institutional leaders offer some certainty in the face of uncertain times.[2]

Assuming a leadership position at a time of major institutional—indeed, social, global, and financial—change has certainly had its challenges: dealing with both public health threats and profound social unrest that play out on my college campus and wider community; making a commitment to antiracism at an institution that has had deep historical investments in white supremacy; and having to create new and ever-evolving arguments for the value of a liberal arts education in an era of the vanishing middle-class and financial vulnerability for a majority of citizens of our nation are no small tasks. But being able to participate in debates and strategic planning for an institution that for over 135 years has provided a transformative education to generations of students is an opportunity and a privilege that I relish. I love my work, even the hard parts.

Notes

[1] Carolyn R. Hodges and Olga M. Welch, *Truth Without Tears: African American Women Deans Share Lessons in Leadership* (Cambridge: Harvard Education Press, 2018).

[2] See https://www.poetryfoundation.org/poems/147275/a-litany-for-survival. Carolyn R. Hodges and Olga M. Welch, "Certainty in Leadership in Uncertain Times." *Inside Higher Ed.* April 17, 2020.

Seven

Something Like a Fresh Start: "Founding" a College of Liberal Arts and Sciences

Frederick J. Antczak

College of Liberal Arts and Sciences at Grand Valley State

Abstract

This is a story about a rare privilege: the opportunity to "found," from existing structures and new visions, a large College of Liberal Arts and Sciences. That opportunity came in the author's home region, in an institution serving many first generation in college students as the author had been. Uniting smaller units under a larger aegis meant creating a new college culture. The story, then, is a constitutive one, about the structures, practices and rituals that gave CLAS at GVSU its fresh start and made it one college. But it is also a personal one, about the ways the author thought about these elements in relation to his having been a first generation in college student, one who had been sustained by skilled advising and mentoring, and been lifted up by extraordinary teaching across disciplines. He had become a professor to extend that opportunity to others, especially to those with less privileged paths to college. This is the story of his becoming a Dean with that commitment as CLAS at GVSU became a college.

Keywords: CLAS, College of Liberal Arts and Sciences, first-generation, deanship, Grand Valley State University, liberal arts, rhetoric, Rhetoric Society of America, service, uberdean, University of Iowa, University of Virginia

***

This is a story of an almost unique, and in retrospect, astonishing privilege. As founding dean of the College of Liberal Arts and Sciences at Grand Valley State University, I was charged in 2004 to help invent a new college, "CLAS." What is more, this opportunity arose in my childhood hometown of Grand Rapids, Michigan, 34 years after I had decamped to pursue my own dream of being a college professor, and was aimed straight at students to whom I had in those decades become particularly dedicated. It flew, moreover, into a brisk professional headwind: colleagues whom I highly respected were bewildered, as if I was choosing to wingsuit off the edge of the known world into an imponderable beyond. Even my mentor, a former dean, at first told me I'd regret it. But my heart became set on being part of a college with that rarest of opportunities in tradition-driven academe: something like a fresh start.

The university was just 40 years into welcoming incoming classes. As such, Grand Valley was the youngest, and therefore least funded per full year equivalent student, among Michigan's 15 public universities. It had had little time to build a reputation, except for good undergraduate teaching. It was due for a fresh start, an internal realignment of scattered smaller administrative units, more in keeping with its rapidly burgeoning size and its consequently more complex mission. Naturally, there were concerns among its faculty about all the indeterminacies that lay ahead, not least this unknown whom some were jokingly calling the "uberdean." Yet what made this job worth taking was a vision of a public university dedicated to liberal education, with a scale of offerings meeting the needs of over 20,000 students, and of a college of liberal arts and sciences tasked to play the largest and most central role within it.

The story, then, is a constitutive one, about the structures, practices and rituals that made us one college. But it is also a personal one, insofar as the ways I thought about these elements in relation to my having been a first-generation in college student, one who had been guided by skilled advising and mentoring, and been lifted up by extraordinary teaching across disciplines. I became a professor, then a dean, to extend that opportunity to others, even to those with less privileged paths to college.

The Firefighter's Kid

I am the son of a firefighter and grandson of a miner, the first in my family to complete college.

Even still, my academic career was festooned with privilege at nearly every turn, with a series of brilliant people stopping to give me a hand up and a direction forward. As an undergraduate at Notre Dame, I had to figure out what children of college-going families—like my roommate, younger brother of a Rhodes Scholar—knew like second nature. But I was in an honors program that assigned me a singularly great advisor, Donald Sniegowski, who led me to a variety of differently brilliant teachers across a range of humanistic areas, and patiently talked me through how I might go about building intellectual bridges between those different disciplines. As a graduate student at the University of Chicago, I cleaved to a magisterial mentor and teacher, Wayne Booth, and was admitted to an interdisciplinary program that permanently opened me up to interdisciplinary learning, the Committee on the Analysis of Ideas and the Study of Methods.

Just weeks after being awarded my PhD, I began my first lecturer job in the Rhetoric Department at the University of California-Berkeley. I saw in my first department chair, Arthur Quinn, what a difference an excellent chair could make, not just for faculty but for students. When the folks on sabbatical began to return and the lecturership ended, Dr. Quinn and other Rhetoric colleagues took time to help me with my applications, and the University of Virginia (UVA) hired me for my first tenure-track job in the Department of Speech Communication, later Rhetoric and Communication Studies.

The years at the University of Virginia were very good to me, so I say this with no bad feeling beyond regret, but they never could grasp what an institutional gem, albeit uncut, they had in the department. I also saw at Virginia the difference a diffident department chair could make. A prominent scholar with ties to administration was brought in from elsewhere. The best that could be said was he learned the names of the faculty, if not many of the students; the worst was that he was unwilling or unable to put his personal capital on the line to make the case for the department. For example, an external review suggested that it was still possible for Virginia, with all its resources, to compete for building the most visible graduate program on the eastern seaboard. But that ball was dropped, and there it lay, among others an able chair might have run with. The young faculty began leaving; the number of majors, which had risen from under 30 to over 300 in five years, then began to plummet. This taught me the administrative meaning of an Emersonian aphorism I had written about in my dissertation, "strike while the iron is hot." I saw that one value an administrator could add was apprising the size of the windows of possibility for good ideas, along with urgency for those windows that were closing. In the long run, the university closed the department, and the chair found his way to a place in one of UVA's excellent, not to say well-appointed, research institutes.

I had landed at the University of Iowa, hired into the Rhetoric Department which was responsible for the roughly 300 sections of basic writing and speaking offered annually to incoming students, and the pedagogical development of the graduate students who taught most of them. These are often regarded as humble tasks in university teaching, and the units dedicated to doing them are sometimes diminished as "service" departments, in much the same way as colleges of arts and sciences are sometimes seen as only sources of such service for the university. But I saw the importance of the work for students and its potential significance for the institution. In due course, I became associated with Iowa's top-ranked Rhetoric and Communication Studies Department, and I began to work with the Project on the Rhetoric of Inquiry (POROI). This group brought together scholars from a variety of disciplines to explore the rhetorics of different disciplines not only in the presentation of their findings, but even in their respective modes of discovery (what ancient rhetoricians identified as the canon of "invention"). POROI's bracing focus on what counted in the academic argument, within Iowa's College of Liberal Arts and Sciences and in other colleges, profoundly affected me. Although always presenting only a local peek at a larger, more complicated canvas—not unlike the glimpses a dean gets—it laid the intellectual groundwork for me to begin to understand disciplinary relationships not just functionally and fiscally, but academically. POROI helped prepare me intellectually for some of the new program building we would do at Grand Valley.

After five years, the job of department chair, at Iowa called "Department Executive Officer," fell to me. I learned a great deal about budgets, and the shifting complexities of schedule-building, juggling 300 sections, the needs of almost 100 graduate student teachers, and my colleagues' requirements and preferences. Perhaps perversely, I always enjoyed working out the puzzle. And I learned optimism from the discovery that, perhaps with the flexibility of others, there was always a solution. More importantly, it really was the first time I felt how administrative power could solve problems that people couldn't solve on their own. Moreover, it permitted me to bring Rhetoric closer to the spotlight, precisely because of its service character. I had a strategy, not wholly original in its scope and leveraging, to hire graduate students to teach the basic writing and speaking course not just from our traditional suppliers—Communication Studies, English, Comparative Literature, the Writers' Workshop—but, when the supply of those candidates was somehow wanting or our standards had risen, from History, Art, Political Science, Philosophy, Classics and the other languages. That in turn spurred more friendly conversations with faculty in those departments who were suddenly more positively disposed to Rhetoric, because they could now support an additional graduate student—all the more when those graduate students came back to their departments from us with exceptional teacher training. These relationships gave me a chance to make our case, often with faculty who did not know us well, and underwrote greater understanding when Rhetoric was involved in proposals before, say, the Educational Policy Committee (EPC) of the college. In time I was elected to the EPC, where I had the privilege of working with Associate Dean for Academic Affairs James Lindberg. Dean Lindberg deserves credit he never felt necessary to take for developing more effective articulation agreements with the state's community colleges and the state's Regents' Institutions. His work in crafting academic policy for a large, complex college informed and enlivened undergraduate education, put it under the light of rigorous review, and adjust it on the run to work even better. His calm was contagious, and his gentleness was a solvent to obstacles. Jim Lindberg is still for me a compelling example of a servant-leader.

But after what then seemed an imponderable fifteen years in his role, he announced that he was stepping down. At the same time, I was ending my second three-year term chairing Rhetoric, and was open to other assignments. I had begun, better late than never, to recognize how lucky I had been. Mindful of the impact my scholarly career could suffer, I nonetheless was more and more conscious of a happy duty to give back. And I was also just curious— administration for me was always an occasion for learning. I applied and got the job.

I had the chance to serve under a smart, tough, fearless, strategic, and more than occasionally funny dean named Linda Maxson, a geneticist who had earned her bones for full professor rank and administrative authority in a generation where that didn't happen easily for women. I learned many things, first that the job was not as easy as Dean Lindberg had made it look. I had much more extensive contact with parents (and delicate relationships with FERPA) than I had had as a department chair. Further, I now had to understand substantive and pedagogical issues far beyond my own discipline. For the first time I served (ex officio) on the college Tenure and Promotion Committee, and saw how portfolios looked to, and might be misunderstood by, audiences outside the home discipline. As a humanist, I learned about startup packages for scientists, the size of which took my breath away, and how skillfully Dean Maxson honed our offers to need. Our "deans' caucuses" exposed me to issues in my fellow associate deans' areas of which I had been ignorant, especially about facilities and equipment needs. It was extraordinary how Dean Maxson helped her associate deans understand the scope and urgencies of problems, but left us going away feeling we were ready to take it on. On top of all of that, she was a good listener, and let us run with ideas with the right amount of background, questions, check-ins and support along the way to meeting clear deadlines. She made me feel like I wanted never to let her down. Altogether, it was a master class in administrator development.

My seventeen years at Iowa afforded me a wonderful array of experiences. The firefighter's son even had the chance to help evacuate our building when the Old Capitol building next door caught fire from its cupola renovation. But to some extent, I had reached a point where I was looking for a new challenge. It was at this point, early in 2004, when I heard about an opening at Grand Valley State University: founding dean of the College of Liberal Arts and Sciences.

Since GVSU had been founded on a campus just 12 miles west of where I grew up in Grand Rapids, Michigan, I had heard of it before. Grand Valley State College had been chartered in 1960 in response to the need for a public four-year university in the state's second-largest metropolitan area. It began graduating classes of about 200 when I was still in high school.

But at that time in its development and mine, I knew Grand Valley did not fit my visions of college very well. When I periodically returned to Grand Rapids to visit my family, I heard about changes in the place from high school classmates who went there, and in the early 1990s I remember my favorite uncle showing off its new downtown campus where a grimy industrial area had once been located. A GVSU faculty member happened to be an Iowa grad on whose PhD committee I had served, so I gave her a call to get her perspective. Still tentative, I submitted my application materials at 4:55 p.m. to an electronic search site that would close at 5:00 p.m.

I already knew the provost, Gayle Davis, had a strong vision that centered the liberal arts and sciences in the enterprise of the university. But the interview was eye-opening. The university was much more extensive than I expected, although physical plant upgrades continued to chase student needs throughout my deanship. Big never scared me. Big can give you economies of scale. But what was really startling was the quality of faculty I met. That's a key part of my personal story that may prove true for other aspiring deans: I came to want the job because the faculty convinced me that the job was worth pursuing. A few of my Iowa colleagues' dire concerns notwithstanding—one of my favorites told me, "well, I admire your pluck"—I had begun to see the possibilities of the Grand Valley deanship as greater than any foreseeably available to me at Iowa. In 100 years, Iowa will still be more or less Iowa, a great flagship university. Grand Valley, however, was still working out what it was going to be, and I saw the chance to influence that with a fresh start for a huge college, with liberal arts and sciences central to the university mission. The job was offered, and I accepted. Little did I know that serving as dean of CLAS at Grand Valley would call on every bit of my experience, from having been a first generation student lifted up by great advising, through having seen the differences a very good and a not so good department chair could make, to the value of service, to the several sorts of interdisciplinarities that could make administration more than a zero-sum game, to the lubricative value of calm and gentleness in a leader, to everyday habits of developing the people you work with.

A Fresh Start for the Liberal Arts and Sciences: Building Unifying Institutions

On July 1, 2004, I became founding dean of the new College of Liberal Arts and Sciences at GVSU. The good news was that I wasn't building from scratch. A "division" of social sciences had existed, as did a "division" of arts and humanities with a vibrant arts area, if fragmented by personal tensions between long-serving leaders, and there was a very large "school" of communication with somewhat different structural roots. And there was a "division" of natural and mathematical sciences, where skepticism about the provost's plan to unify under a single dean seemed to be the highest. Holding the new concept together for me was a faculty dedicated to a genuinely shared priority on teaching. The bad news was that on Day One, I would be responsible for distributing something like 300,000 student credit hours—nobody quite knew, exactly—to meet the burgeoning and shifting needs of the wildly growing student body, enlisting and directing the efforts of over 400 tenure-track faculty, scores of adjuncts hired in a bountiful variety of ways but supervised in fewer, and a stretched support staff that had seen its responsibilities explode in magnitude as the student body had grown. Adding a degree of difficulty, the former divisions had each done tenure and promotion a little differently, reviewed curriculum a little differently and, surprisingly, kept the books a little differently and assigned course loads differently. What I saw in those differences were many efficiencies that could be realized. In time, we would take good ideas from every corner of the former divisions and fearlessly propagate them.

But there was a prior, more fundamental task: the essential work would be in unifying the college—getting faculty and staff to think of themselves as members of CLAS, and contributing to its enterprise. Doing so would require reinventing collegiate administration and governance to comprise all of the liberal arts and sciences, and creating collegiate events, rituals and practices that would lead to a collegiate identity—I wanted to use this fresh start to build a college that faculty and staff felt was a thing held in common. But this situatedness in time, circumstance and community makes me add a caution. What follows is how I thought it through at GVSU, 2004-2020. To apply these principles elsewhere would require a new and differently adapted deployment.

The associate deans my provost had appointed for me were very strong, but their duties had been arranged one each per former division. This setup would be effective in creating a certain kind of interdisciplinary entity I had seen before: a federation, three populations alongside each other that held little in common besides the dean (positioned in this conception to function as the uberdean of last resort). But a federation retained all the same motives of mutual competition, and offered far fewer of the occasions of talking each other's language and appealing to each other's values. I believed that we could learn from and strengthen each other, and that the former clumps of departments did not constitute indissolubly separate interests. So, by the second year I had realigned the decanal duties as associate dean for faculty, associate dean for students and curriculum, and associate dean for facilities, space and faculty development. All issues involving faculty went through one associate dean; one associate dean was the first stop for all student issues and for curricular development across the disciplines; and our material needs, great as they were as student numbers continued to grow faster than facilities and equipment, went through one process and one person. My job was to help my associate deans shape the processes in their respective areas of responsibility, so that appeals and submissions from various departments were comparable, and had the information necessary to balance them within always scarce resources. This brought clarity quickly: for example, it was plain that Grand Valley was becoming a much more popular destination for the whole range of pre-health majors, and we were able to compile data that let me make the case not only to our provost but to other faculty, justifying faculty lines, equipment, facilities, a building renovation, and ultimately a new building. At the same time, we were able to identify equipment needs in the performing arts, and justify the shifting of college funds to meet needs. This was hardly an original realization, but a good example of one that faculty in other departments needed to hear—that the arts, and particularly music, constituted a special kind of outreach. There are portions of the public that may never be able to see or assess a university's program in biochemistry, engineering, the health professions, but they know what they like when they hear it. With more faculty and more instruments, the arts could not only make us all look good, but could dispose our various audiences in a way that made our other excellences more recognizable.

The associate dean jobs shape-shifted over time, and the dean's office—I tried ineffectively to get people to call it "the college O\office"—expanded in services and people. I had an assistant dean for budget, whose job, she said, was to help me "find where all the bodies were buried"; in one of the divisions, there were many, but one by one we disinterred these arrangements up into the light of day, and addressed them as the college needed in the new moment. That job grew over time in the depth and range of analysis, especially as grant work grew, becoming an assistant dean for finance and project management. A later associate dean for facilities brought his expertise in analytics, and took on responsibilities for promoting research as well. The associate dean for faculty took on responsibilities for planning. It is worth noting that the cross-disciplinary nature of each of the associate deanships prepared people for next career steps. Currently, two former associate deans are now deans elsewhere, two are provosts, and one is a president.

One thing that did not shift was that all the deans continued to teach and do normal faculty duties as part of their assignments. My philosophy was that leaders go with everyone else, without special exceptions. I taught the least often, about once every three years, courses ranging from graduate seminars in English to first year writing. In years I did not teach, I was occupied with national service as executive director of the Rhetoric Society of America, and managed to continue to publish in dribbles. The associate deans' appointments always dedicated some portion of their workload to teaching. For as difficult as those semesters were, they bought lots of street cred, and friendly parking lot conversations about how our teaching was going. It's good almost anytime deans are included in any reference to "our."

Advising got my particular attention. Over most of my sixteen years, we served a student body that had some of the same shortfalls in cultural capital I had suffered. And for some, it was a shortfall of actual capital: as one of my students put it, "I have to work 30 or 35 hours a week. College is my second job." My memories went back to Notre Dame, and all the things I didn't know that were second nature to second-gen students. The science division had built a small tutoring center; under Betty Schaner, a brilliant and dedicated director, later Assistant Dean for Student Academic Services and Advising, we retooled it to stretch professional advising across the disciplines. Later the CLAS Advising Center also took a central role in the summer orientation of new students. I worked closely with Director Schaner on articulation agreements with Michigan's community colleges, and learned most about their institutional challenges and how we could make life simpler for our students in common from a duo of exceptional administrators at Grand Rapids Community College, Laurie Chesley and Michael Vargo.

Our Director for Communication and Advancement, Monica Johnstone, helped invent a staff advisory committee, an alumni board, other consultative committees, and events from a golf tournament benefitting CLAS Scholarships to a repair clinic to which students could bring torn backpacks and worn clothes to stretch out usability. She worked with me to set up a small discretionary fund, enough to underwrite the degree of flexibility important for any new dean. She also helped me understand and handle an endemic PR (public relations) problem of colleges of liberal arts and sciences. University Communication offices have a remarkable way of finding headline stories in the new supply chain major that will produce 10 students a year, or in the latest program of similar size in engineering or health professions. To be sure, they are stories, they are news; but such offices seem to have endemic difficulties "sizing them up" in comparison with programs that are producing hundreds of immediately hireable, albeit versatile, graduates. The public knows what a nurse or accountant does; the problem is getting them to hear about and appreciate graduates who can do many things like a liberal arts grad can. The Director of Communication and Advancement—a Rhetoric PhD with a decade of experience with industry—played a key role in keeping us visible within the university and beyond it. Collaborating with her, we developed internal communication too, in the forms of a weekly mailing with a calendar, and a monthly e-magazine, *CLAS Acts*, that enabled us to tell the stories of both opportunities and accomplishments. And, importantly for a college with scarce resources, one of the currencies in which CLAS capitalized itself with was, simply, glory—the publicity, cordons, plaques and awards that made people feel their efforts were seen and appreciated.

As wonderful as our associate deans have been, the importance of department chairs and directors could not be overstated. Mindful of the difference that able, engaged chairs could make, we put serious resources into department chair diversity, recruitment, and development. Because of our scale—25 departments,

527 tenure-track FTE (full-time equivalent), and 360,000 student credit hours—
we were able to do a vigorous "New Unit Head Orientation" with continuing
professional development. We always sent new unit heads to CCAS's new
department chair seminars, and I sequestered a special fund for their professional
development. I believe it is the most difficult position in the university.

In governance too, we needed to braid together the best ideas from the former
divisions. Before I arrived, I did my best to find out who were the most respected
members of the faculty and, making sure to include department chairs and
people who had served at different levels of divisional and university governance,
I appointed a committee of six to draft a proposal for the college bylaws on
which the whole faculty could vote. I gave them only a timeline, and a request
that one of the committees be somehow explicitly devoted to faculty development.
It was at this point that a member of the committee, echoing the concern about
an uberdean, asked me if I intended to chair the committee. The members were
surprised and relieved that I neither intended to chair, nor attend their
deliberations except when invited. One new colleague told me that there had
been concerns that a new dean, fresh off 25 years at prestigious R-1 institutions,
would conduct himself as the smartest guy in the room. I responded that if I
ever found myself the smartest guy in a room, I'd be pretty sure that I was in the
wrong room. I saw deanship not as managing faculty and staff to an administrative
agenda I imposed, but empowering them to collaborate, with the informational
resources they needed, and moving along on the schedule by which the university
required a decision. That didn't mean I wouldn't describe limitations or critique
ideas; it meant that my ideas would be stated after others', and would have to
stand the same level of interrogation as anyone else's. When my behavior over
time proved consistent with this approach, the concern over an uberdean
began to abate.

The drafting committee proposed four governance committees: Personnel,
Curriculum, Faculty Development, and a Faculty Council (a hybrid of a faculty
assembly and an executive committee, specifically in charge of the college bylaws, elections and other constitutive matters). These were small committees,
assuring that each member was responsible for representing something larger
than one discipline. Each committee was chaired by a faculty member, and had
an ex officio associate dean or dean member. Within only a couple of years—
and thanks in large amount to the gifted faculty leaders who stepped forward
to chair these faculty committees and shape their cultures—they became
second nature. It became amazingly normal to have a musician interrogate a
course proposal by the Statistics Department, to have a professor of ancient
languages examine equipment proposals or line requests from Chemistry, or to
have a mathematician vote on the tenure and promotion of a dancer, or an
expert in constitutional law. As a rhetorician, I could not help but notice that

over the years, lines of discussion and reasoning changed, to be less closed down in the ostensibly unquestionable authority of the department, and more open to citizenship in the community we were making together in the college. At the same time the inventiveness grew, usually on faculty initiative, if occasionally on my dime. For example, the Faculty Development Committee began supporting workshops for sabbatical proposal writing. Faculty Council invented "out of the box lunches" and events on topics ranging from interdisciplinary "research clusters" to "collaborative teaching" to resources for "faculty as first responders" to "getting your groove back."

Tenure and promotion decisions moved towards this ideal most deliberately. The process was greatly aided by my provost's wise request that academic units write explicit promotion guidelines. I framed that request as not to describe the lowest bar a candidate could shinny over and yet be deserving of pre-tenure renewal, tenure and promotion to associate, or full professor; but instead to describe what a clearly promotable candidate looks like—something aspirational, not formulaic. The faculty came through, and the guidelines were edited, vetted, and approved up the line. After that, judgments of the dean and the personnel committee converged—no small task when we were seeing upwards of 50 candidates a year. Differences in my final five years were very few in number, and usually concerned how many years of renewal sent the right message.

But if administration and governance were moving toward an operationally shared vision of the college as a commonly held and mutually built and continuously rebuilt artifact, what could give the faculty and staff a sense of belonging within it?

Belonging: Ritual and Recognition

Drawing again on an existing idea and scaling it up, I set up our college's very first fall start up meeting in our biggest theater, followed by a picnic for 800, literally under a "Big Top." This meeting had an agenda built to make all sorts of people feel they belonged. First, we introduced new faculty and their areas of teaching and scholarship; these introductions resulted in a number of cross-disciplinary collaborations over the years. Then we honored faculty who had been promoted to associate and full professor. In time, we included awards for "contribution in a discipline." We gave cordons for teaching awards, and after a few years, differently colored and braided cordons to those faculty who had chaired one of the governance committees. I spoke, outlining the themes and goals for the year. And then the president and provost visited, as they did every college, with their overarching messages. Finally, we always had a musical performance by our faculty. Then we held a picnic under a rented "Big Top" on the theory that if my speechifying couldn't quite suffice to attract people, food might just help. We would walk over to the tent together, but in the year our usual area had been taken for the new library, I impressed the marching band to lead us to our new spot. Since we needed to cross a ravine and since hundreds of people marching could create a harmonic motion that threatened structural integrity, I became the only dean I know to instruct his faculty to *get out of* step.

During the week before fall semester exams, we held a casual lunch in our student union. It was also the occasion for the college to give each of its staff a small present—something like a little blanket, or a "cooler cup," branded of course with the college logo. The recipients were grateful to be remembered, and everyone was glad to get away from grading for lunch. The event had student guitar music, and was punctuated by a student ensemble performing holiday music in the building's atrium for student and faculty passersby. Regrettably, near the end of my decanal service, my new provost asked us to cut this event. The appearances were wrong for a time of austerity and budget-cutting. I reluctantly complied. But I still mourn the loss of a relatively affordable event that, in a week of stress, contributed greatly to the sense that we were a community, and not just a place you put in your eight hours and go straight home. I would argue that it paid for itself in a more valuable currency of connection and dedication. I hope for the day that something like it—something different, something better—may return.

In late March or early April we staged our sabbatical showcase. Twenty to thirty-five faculty recently returned from sabbatical did posters or other performances of their sabbatical outcomes, emphasizing scholarship but including payoffs for teaching and community engagement. Humanists were slow to the party, but an extraordinary poster by historian Grace Coolidge helped break that logjam for good. Faculty learned about what constituted scholarly argument in different disciplines—I heard echoes of my Iowa POROI experience—and these discussions resulted in many teaching and scholarly collaborations. Over the years, members of other colleges, the president and provost, the public, alumni, a couple of legislators, and more than a few trustees toured the exhibits—your tax dollars impressively at work, in a college where the public doesn't expect such practical payoffs. There was food, and while all were seated we had a short program. There were awards for staff, and for service, which faculty had always felt went underrecognized. Both of these categories recognized accomplishment in the calendar year past, and lifetime achievement. There were reports from each of the governance committees, and I spoke about what had been done, and what it meant, in the context of the goals I had articulated in the fall. And of course there was music.

Reflections

When in May 2019 I announced that 2019-2020 would be my last year as dean before returning to faculty status to teach and write, we had become a very different college. Our processes were integrated, our internal and external communication honed, our fundraising bolstered, our faculty development (as well as our development of talented administrators) flourishing, our research and scholarship increased in scope and elevated in influence, and our teaching, especially in the mentorship of undergraduate student scholarship, enhanced by facilities, resources and recognition. This had not happened without failings, certainly not without my failings. Nor did it result from vast infusions of state funds; indeed, the student numbers grew far faster than state support, while Grand Valley State University, mindful of its mission of access, was very disciplined in its tuition increases. It was partially a story of skillful central administrators, particularly a provost with guts and a clear institutional vision, and the crazy faith to let me work on it. It was decidedly not a story of an uberdean, although I hope it turned out in some measure to be a story of a Dean-mit-Alles, for as I had learned from Iowa's legendary Professor Sam Becker, "the highest rank in the university is full professor; anything else is just an assignment." But it was mostly the story of an academic community enlivened by its dedication to students, and enriched by a robustly cross-disciplinary concept of the liberal arts and sciences. CLAS at Grand Valley State University is a remarkable success story because of the willingness of people to work together and to collaborate on a fresh start.

Eight

The Inside Track: Becoming Dean at your Home Institution

Bonnie Gunzenhauser

John Carroll University

Abstract

Large organizations in the 21st century - universities included - need a multidimensional approach to hiring for leadership positions. Both theory and practice affirm that there are plenty of good reasons to hire new talent with new perspectives from outside a university when the time comes to find the next dean or provost, but there are also real benefits to considering internal candidates for these positions. In this essay, I will discuss the strategies that I found useful in starting a decanal role at the same institution where I earned tenure and served as a faculty member for a decade, as well as some of tactics internal hires may want to consider as they step into a new role at a (seemingly) familiar institution.

Keywords: best practices, community, cultural translator, dark side, deanship, home institution, growth mindset, inside track, institutional culture, institutional knowledge, leader, listening tour, messy middle, network, organizational change trajectory, portable skills, professional development, shared governance, strategies, translation

***

There are multiple pathways to a deanship. Colleges and universities, like most large and complex organizations, have good reasons to take a multidimensional, "build and buy" approach to hiring administrators, looking internally and externally at different times for different reasons.[1] Both routes to a deanship come with particular possibilities and pitfalls, for the candidate and for the hiring institution. An external hire creates an opportunity for a college or university to reflect on current priorities and to develop an intentional profile of the kind of leader who will help to build the desired future, while an internal hire comes with a less steep learning curve, an internal network of relationships, and tested institutional knowledge and commitment.[2] In this essay, I will discuss strategies that I found useful in starting a decanal role at the same institution where I earned tenure and served as a faculty member for a decade, as well as some things internal hires may want to consider as they step into a new role at a (seemingly) familiar institution.

Early in my career, as I was making final revisions to a scholarly project several years in the making, a colleague advised: "Now you need to look at the whole thing with the cold, fishy eye of the stranger." More easily said than done, but the basic idea was wise: I needed to defamiliarize something I thought I knew well in order to achieve the best possible result. When I became dean at the institution where I had already spent ten years as a faculty member, department chair, and associate dean, this piece of advice came back to me. Certainly, after ten years I knew my colleagues, I knew our students, I knew our programs and our points of distinction, I reasoned. Did that turn out to be true? Yes. And no. The eye I brought during those first months in the deanship might not have been cold and fishy exactly, but I did spend my first few months behaving, as much as possible, as if I were new to the place.

So, what did this look like? Most broadly, it meant approaching people and programs with what Carol Dweck calls a "growth mindset."[3] Such a mindset may come naturally – most educators instinctively look for ways to grow and develop—but after many years in the same context, and with a much broader unit now in your charge, it may take some conscious effort to fully adopt this approach on an institutional scale. For me, starting with a growth mindset meant getting intensely curious about every aspect of the college—the traditional start-up "listening tour" is absolutely as important for internal hires as for external ones. I knew my colleagues, to varying degrees, as peers from assorted regular meetings, but I had never had the occasion to really delve into their particular corner of the university, and to ask all kinds of questions about their unit's personnel, programs, aspirations, conflicts, and concerns. These conversations were uniformly illuminating for me. I was reminded, time and again, about how individualized, and even isolating, faculty life can be, and thus realized early on that one key imperative for me would be to consciously and continually look for ways to build a meaningful community. During these conversations, I also learned many things about the challenges and accomplishments of my colleagues that had been invisible to me as a peer, and only became visible because I defamiliarized myself and explored rather than assumed I knew the context I'd inherited. I think these conversations were reassuring to my colleagues as well, because they demonstrated that I wasn't going to rely on my own (no doubt partial and imperfect) preconceptions, but instead was willing to take the time to get to know them again, for the first time.

Perhaps less inspiring, but equally important, these conversations also exposed previously invisible departmental rifts and conflicts. I suspect (based not simply on personal experience, but on conversations with scores of decanal colleagues through the years) that almost every institution has at least one or two units that air no dirty laundry publicly but that stymie collective forward motion because of decades-old grudges and sore spots. These units are challenging to deal with no matter what—but they're impossible to deal with if you don't know they exist. So, it's important to ask your colleagues not just about the many wonderful things that are happening with their units' teaching, research, programming, and outreach activities; you also want to ask some probing questions about internal politics to help you manage and lead effectively.

If you've become dean at your home institution, you've almost certainly already built a track record of effective management and leadership, perhaps as a department chair, or program director, or associate dean. As such, you have some undeniable built-in advantages in terms of institutional knowledge, familiarity with the student body's strengths and needs, and, presumably, some strong networks of support and trust. Recent research on organizational culture indicates that in some ways you may be better positioned for success than an external hire, because "hiring organizations tend to overestimate the 'portability' of skills and experience—how quickly and effectively they can be applied in new organizations."[4] However, there is one asset you can never have: you can't be new. This reality presents some challenges to be aware of as you step into the role. For one thing, you have an institutional history—you've done things, you've made decisions, you've taken positions on issues—and these realities may lead some of your colleagues to make assumptions (both positive and negative) about how you'll respond to any future initiative. Here too, perhaps the best way to move past these preconceptions is to be intentional and explicit about your efforts to create as clean a slate as possible. Seek information from many sources (remember that you will have access to some different information by virtue of your new role), be willing to re-evaluate prior positions on the basis of this new information, and be open about the fact that you are approaching your new role with fresh eyes, and that, as you embrace your wider purview, your views may evolve.[5]

One way to clean your slate, or at least to broaden your perspective, is to be purposeful about your professional development from day one—or sooner. Consider asking your institution to invest in your attendance at one of the industry-standard leadership development programs as part of your hiring package. These programs (whether through CCAS, the Harvard Graduate School of Education, the HERS Institute, or another industry organization) provide terrific management and leadership advice, as well as valuable surveys of current industry trends. Equally important, they create instant professional networks that you can draw on as you navigate your new role.[6] Institutions seek external hires in part because they perceive them as having valuable outsider knowledge that will speed the organization's change trajectory. With this kind of professional development under your belt, you'll step into your role with some of these external resources already in place, and will have alternative perspectives and real-world models to offer both in forward-looking planning activities and in response to the inevitable "we've always done it this way!" objections that will arise as you begin to consider and implement change.

Getting serious about your professional development can also help you to be a transformational actor at an institution in which you're already deeply invested. The knowledge of industry-level best practices and paradigms you'll build through professional development will give an early boost to your credibility and effectiveness as a leader. Then, with that new baseline, you will have a tremendous opportunity to leverage your insider knowledge and serve both your college and the institution as, essentially, a cultural translator. When you begin the deanship, you'll encounter a cast of characters in senior leadership roles with whom you will likely have had little prior occasion to interact. Given how often institutions hire externally for these roles – one recent study indicates that 80% of college presidents are external hires – many of these leaders will be relatively new to the institution, and you may be one of the few long-time insiders that they have occasion to talk with regularly and to know well.[7] As such, you have a crucial role to play. These leaders are often hired to develop new strategic plans, point the university in new directions, and to otherwise disrupt the status quo. This disruption can be valuable and necessary, but often these leaders also face tremendous pressure to make change quickly and lack ready access to reliable information about institutional history and faculty culture. As an internal hire who has developed expertise in industry best practices, as well as lived expertise in the resources (human and other) of your institution, you are uniquely positioned to contextualize and advocate in ways that will help these recently-arrived campus leaders to minimize missteps and maximize institutional strengths in the process of making change. If, as Elizabeth Lehfeldt observes, "increasingly, there seems to be a class of professional administrators . . . [which] creates a situation where proximity and insider knowledge are in short supply," then as a leader who came up on the inside track, you have a tremendous opportunity to leverage your proximity and insider knowledge for the benefit of all.[8]

As an inside hire, then, cultural translation may be an important part of your work managing up. I found it equally useful, though, also to think of myself as a cultural translator in my work of managing "down."[9] One great strength you bring to the role as an internal hire is your credibility within the network of internal relationships you've built during your pre-administrative years. While there may be a few members of that network who will assume you've made an instant and irreversible Jekyll-to-Hyde transformation when you move into administration, most of your colleagues will appreciate having someone they perceive as understanding their perspective working on their behalf within the larger institutional culture. This is the perfect precondition for cultural translation. We've probably all seen dedicated and long-serving faculty members dismiss newly hired, change-minded senior leaders and their decisions as peremptory or ill-advised. While it is decidedly not your role to be an unquestioning apologist for your administrative colleagues, you may be able to help translate valid but potentially controversial leadership moves to your faculty colleagues in ways that make the logic more persuasive. This translation may be situational, about a particular initiative or decision. But it may also be more existential: as an internal hire with a growth mindset, some professional development, and expanding external networks, you have an opportunity to help some colleagues imagine the possibility that they might revisit their preconceptions and perhaps even take a similar route themselves.

These colleagues may at first greet with mock (or actual) horror the idea of "crossing over," as it's so often put, to "the dark side." But as a faculty insider who crossed over and (presumably) retained your soul, you have some unique credibility with which to counter this "dark side" rhetoric—and, I would argue, there is considerable value in doing so. As a number of commentators have observed recently, there are real institutional costs to what may seem like a gently sardonic trope.

> It lets faculty members dismiss the work and decisions of the administration out of hand simply because they come from the administrative side. It implicitly encourages administrators to see faculty members as the enemy by positing that when we move from faculty to administration we become different creatures who abandon any of our previous faculty priorities and sensibilities. But as with so many dichotomies, it is a false construct; reality resides somewhere in the messy middle.[10]

That messy middle is where deans live – and, as an internal hire who came up among the faculty and who now spends considerable time with the administrative other, your ability to bridge the gap is considerable. You are one version of a lived answer to the question George Justice and Carolyn Dever pose in their "From the Dark Side" series: "What would it mean to assume that significant administrative service should be part of a strong, healthy and fulfilling faculty career?"[11]

This question merits serious consideration. At a moment when colleges and universities are embattled on any number of external fronts – unfavorable demographic trends, public disinvestment both affective and financial—it seems particularly critical to move toward greater mutual understanding internally. There are natural disagreements between faculty and administrators: conflicting views over immediate priorities, future directions, and where to invest increasingly scarce resources are inevitable (though it's worth noting that neither group likely has a monolithic position on these issues either). But as someone who has already gone some way to bridge the faculty-administrator divide in your own career, you have a platform to help your colleagues think about commonalities across the two domains—at a minimum, to build stronger mutual understanding, and perhaps, to encourage some of your colleagues to see a move from faculty to administration as a step along a continuum rather than a leap across a yawning chasm. In a classic *Harvard Business Review* study, John P. Kotter suggests that most managerial roles involve two main activities: first, "figuring out what to do despite uncertainty and an enormous amount of potentially relevant information," and, second, "getting things done through a large and diverse group of people despite having little direct control over most of them."[12] Kotter conducted his analysis with senior leaders across a range of industries—but these activities sound strikingly similar to a good deal of faculty work. What is developing a syllabus or designing a research project if not charting a path through "an enormous amount of potentially relevant information"? What is a commitment to operating through a robust model of shared governance if not a belief in "getting things done through a large and diverse group of people despite having little direct control over most of them"? A shared methodology does not necessarily lead to shared conclusions, but it does suggest a place to start: namely, with the insight that faculty and administrators share some core values in terms of how to approach the thorny problems that they confront in their respective – and mutual – domains.

As someone who has likely recognized these common approaches, whether implicitly or explicitly, you can contribute to the overall health of your institution by focusing part of your leadership energies on catalyzing increased internal leadership development. It probably isn't healthy or desirable for all new leaders to come from within, but neither is it healthy or desirable for an institution to be without strong options for internal succession in at least some key roles. By investing some of your time, energy, and resources in identifying and mentoring potential leaders within your organization, you may be able not just to strengthen your institution but, arguably, help to develop a healthier paradigm for faculty-administrator relations within higher education.[13]

A final thought: as I write this essay, I have recently left the institution where I spent seventeen years as faculty member and dean to begin a new deanship at a new institution. As I settle into the new position, I'm grateful for my insider experience: the learning curve of the deanship was substantial when I started at my home institution, but the learning curve for the institution overall was smaller. Now, as I begin my new deanship, I find the situation reversed: I have a good stockpile of decanal experience on which to draw, but I need to learn the institution in order to discern what parts of that stockpile might make sense here, and in what ways. What strikes me in making this shift from insider to outsider is this: effective academic leadership requires broad knowledge, *and* it is highly context dependent. I do believe that inside hires have a special role to play in bridging the faculty-administrator divide – but I also believe that, whether you arrive at the deanship via an inside track, or from a different institution altogether, you will be most effective if you approach the role with an appreciation for the generative possibilities that come from keeping a dynamic tension between depth and breadth, local culture and (inter)national context, front and center in all that you do.

Notes

[1] Rita O'Donnell, "Understanding Talent's 'Build or Buy' Conundrum," *HR Dive*, April 22, 2019.
[2] Two useful thought-pieces on the issue of internal and external hires in academic administration are Lucy Apthorp Leske, "Hiding in Plain Sight," *Inside Higher Ed.*, June 8, 2009, and Nathan Bennett, "Our Leader Left. Who's Left to Lead?," *The Chronicle of Higher Education*, July 22, 2015.
[3] Carol Dweck, *Mindset: The New Psychology of Success* (New York: Random House Publishing, 2006).
[4] Krell, Eric, "Weighing Internal vs. External Hires," *HR Magazine*, January 7, 2015.
[5] Leibovich, Mark, "You and I Change our Minds: Politicians 'Evolve,'" *New York Times Magazine*, March 10, 2015.
[6] Trisalyn Nelson and Jessica Early, "How to Counter the Isolation of Academic Life," *The Chronicle of Higher Education*, February 2, 2020. The authors argue persuasively that, for all academics—faculty and administrator alike—"your ecosystem needs to be diverse, especially as you advance in your career."
[7] Thomas J. Pfaff, "Getting the Big Hires Right," *Inside Higher Ed.*, June 26, 2019.
[8] Elizabeth A. Lehfeldt, "Crossing Over," *Inside Higher Ed.*, February 18, 2015.
[9] For a recent useful guide to strategies and approaches to this kind of multidimensional management, see *The HBR Guide to Managing Up and Across* (Boston: Harvard Business Review Press, 2013).
[10] Elizabeth Lehfeldt, "Stop Calling it the Dark Side," *Inside Higher Ed.*, June 14, 2017.
[11] George Justice and Carolyn Dever, "Beyond the Dark Side," *Inside Higher Ed.*, May 16, 2019.
[12] John P. Kotter, "What Effective General Managers Really Do," *Harvard Business Review* 77:2 (March-April 1999): 148.

[13] Elizabeth Lehfeldt makes some excellent suggestions for ways to do this in "In Our Own Backyards." *Inside Higher Ed.*, June 16, 2016.

Nine

The Seemingly Small Matters that Shape Our Future: Timely Questions, Epiphanies, and Saying Yes to Opportunities

Karen Petersen

University of Tulsa

Abstract

Perhaps more than at any time, good leadership is crucial for the future of higher education, particularly in the arts and sciences. Rather than looking for candidates whose trajectory matches that which we expect, I posit that my non-traditional background and path to leadership prepared me well for the ongoing challenges facing our disciplines as well as for the COVID crisis. Having a strong sense of purpose, clear ethical boundaries, and humility are far more important for leadership than the right credentials or experiences. Furthermore, increased diversity could be an additional benefit of focusing less on the typical path to leadership.

Keywords: administration, best practices, core values, COVID-19, crisis response team, emotional intelligence, first-generation, Kendall College of Arts and Sciences, leadership, liberal arts, Middle Tennesee State University, morale, personnel issues, politics, relationships, soft skills, strategic planning, student enrollment, University of Tulsa, Vanderbilt

***

"What do you want to do with your life?" While I still have no single answer to that question, I can say with certainty that being asked changed my life. When Jack Turner addressed that question to me at the end of class in my junior year of college, I had no idea that one could make a living trading in ideas. As a first-generation college student who did not complete high school, I told him that I needed to get a real job. He told me I could get paid to continue my education, and, as I often tell my students, I never looked back.

Although my mentors in my PhD program at Vanderbilt encouraged me to pursue a research career, I wanted to do for students what Jack Turner had done for me. I made it my mission to change lives by caring about students enough to ask questions. I returned to my alma mater, Middle Tennessee State University (MTSU), to serve students who would otherwise not have access to higher education and to give them the highest quality experience possible. In this, I excelled.

Like most junior faculty, I set my sights on tenure and went to work. Unlike many tenure-track faculty, I engaged immediately in the politics of the department without fear. My experience in graduate school coincided with an extremely contentious and toxic period for the department, during which I learned that keeping one's head down and failing to advocate for your own well-being and your colleagues did nothing to protect you and came at a high cost. I spoke up for my fellow students when they would not, met with administrators to advocate for the protection of graduate students in the program, and secured some small wins for our group. My peers asked me to do so, and I was too naïve to say no. In the process, I learned a lot of lessons about leadership from terrible examples—lessons that would become the bedrock for my work. In particular: do what is right and treat people well.

I did not enter the academy with the intention of becoming an administrator. In fact, I call myself an "accidental administrator" and try to avoid hiring people whose goal is to be in administration. I have found that those who really love being faculty members, who also care about the governance of the institution, make superior administrators. Instead, I suspect we often hire those who do not particularly enjoy the faculty role and want a way out or, God forbid, actually think that they will have power as administrators.

I became a part-time assistant dean because someone I like and respect asked me to take charge of assessment and retention. Neither of those issues was particularly meaningful to me, but I saw the opportunity as essentially without risk, given that I would continue to teach, research, and serve as a faculty member while taking on some new tasks. I discovered quickly that I enjoyed being out of my department and getting to know colleagues across the college and that I was quite good at finding creative ways to make assessment work (or make it less painful) by finding means to assess student learning that actually fit with the disciplinary norms. It was in this role that I discovered my strengths and weaknesses in emotional intelligence and began to work on my soft skills.

When the associate dean retired, I applied for her position and was selected for that role, which brought me into the dean's office full-time. I accepted the position with the caveat that I would still be able to teach one class each year and co-lead an education abroad trip in the summer. I have observed that administrators who leave the classroom permanently often lose touch with the mission, become resentful of faculty, and fail to find fulfillment in their work.

Although I did not train for administration or leadership, my background as a political scientist brought with it a set of skills that have been critically important as an administrator. I am not intimidated by data. In fact, I enjoy working with data and strive to inform all important decisions with both quantitative and qualitative data. I know how to read, write, and understand policy. I can communicate complex ideas to a diverse audience. Most important, of course, I know how to learn. The first assignment I was given was to "do a strategic plan" for the college. I read several books about strategic planning and developed an approach that took into account best practices but allowed for the creativity and diversity of the liberal arts to inform our work. I also began reading about leadership.[1]

The variety of tasks I assumed from day-to-day expanded dramatically. This is perhaps the single most substantive difference between faculty life and administrative life. Faculty life, at least for me, became routine: work on the same research area, teach the same classes, attend meetings that seemed to have the same basic rhythm regardless of purpose, and answer the same questions from different students. It's a great life; I'm convinced those who fail to appreciate it have never had another job. However, I will admit that I was restless after achieving tenure. Moving to administration and keeping one toe in the classroom energized me. I love to learn, and I had to become knowledgeable on a staggering variety of topics: curriculum, budgets, physical resources, advising, and more. As anyone who has served in a leadership role can attest, I also had to become an expert on people. Personnel issues are the most vexing, potentially fraught, and rewarding issues we tackle in our daily work. This is where the liberal arts uniquely prepares leaders to succeed. The skills we develop in our disciplines prepare us well to lead, if we can add humility to those skills and if we have a baseline of integrity upon which to build our leadership profile.

In addition to the responsibilities typically assigned to an associate dean, I participated in university-wide leadership in areas that interested me, volunteered for a variety of tasks, and invested in my own professional development. Although I had no grand plan for my career, I felt like I was on a new path with a lot of possible jumping-off points. I wanted to learn as much as possible about higher education and leadership because these areas interested me and because experience taught me that opportunities would come along when I was not looking for them. I wanted to be prepared.

When the dean of liberal arts was asked to serve as provost, he asked me to step into the deanship in an interim capacity. At that point, I had fewer than three years of experience as associate dean. However, during that time, he included me in nearly every aspect of his work—partly because he valued my insights and partly, I assume, to prepare me for my next role. Whatever his motivation, the confidence he placed in me, the honesty with which we interacted, his willingness to provide critical feedback and accept the same formed the most effective mentoring experience I could imagine. I will always be grateful for his willingness to invest in my success and would not be where I am today without those experiences. As such, I have tried to do the same with my team.

While there is a certain amount of formality expected of a dean, I decided that I could benefit a lot from the expertise of the 350+ people who make up the faculty and staff of the college. To do that, I needed to be accessible. I also felt the pressure of leading well as the first woman to hold the position in our college. I spent almost two years in an interim role before participating in a national search for the position and shedding the interim title. Unfortunately, my tenure in the dean's office coincided perfectly with a dramatic decline in enrollment in the liberal arts. When I became interim dean, we were hemorrhaging students, faculty morale was low, and the institution always seemed one misstep away from catastrophe. I did not have time to act like an interim, so I decided to do what was best for the college and not worry about the costs to me professionally. We needed to keep moving forward and could not reach our goals if I decided to maintain the status quo to avoid alienating people so that I would be acceptable when a search was conducted.

At this point, another fortuitous question shaped my trajectory. I encountered a colleague from physics in the parking lot who, upon learning I was interim dean of liberal arts, asked me if I spent the day painting. He really had no idea what my colleagues and I did every day, despite the fact that we educated nearly every student on campus by providing more than 50% of the general education student credit hours (SCH) and 30% of the SCH overall. I was stunned, so I gathered a small team of faculty and staff to engage in a branding campaign highlighting the value of a liberal arts education. In many respects, I learned a lot about my own education when forced to articulate its value broadly and coherently, and telling that story became my purpose. I enjoyed advocating for the arts, humanities, and social sciences to various audiences and was willing to talk to anyone who would listen in any format.

We began that campaign internally with the help of our marketing office and support from the provost and president, which leads to another tremendous benefit of administrative work and an absolutely critical component of success: relationships. By this time, I had more than a decade of experience at MTSU, so I knew a lot of people. Although I fail on occasion, I make an effort to treat everyone with respect and value them as human beings over and above their potential to contribute to my success. I believe that complex organizations flourish when people feel valued and know that their work matters. My colleagues beyond liberal arts wanted to help us communicate our mission creatively and effectively. Without the support of many people across campus, we would not have succeeded in telling a compelling story. Our success helped us to boost faculty morale and increase incoming student enrollment. Combined with improvements in retention, we began to grow our programs again. We were succeeding in our effort to build a thriving liberal arts program at a regional public university, and then crisis hit.

In the first week of March 2020, Nashville experienced a major tornado outbreak, followed days later by the recognition that COVID-19 was going to alter our lives radically very quickly. I happened to be attending a seminar on crisis leadership at the Harvard Kennedy School of Government that week, which prepared me well to return to campus and shift to crisis leadership. It was during the early weeks of the crisis that I realized how well prepared I was to lead through the challenges. I was prepared because I spent a lot of time learning and, most critical, I had hired a core group of excellent, trustworthy people to work alongside me.

My crisis response team included two associate deans, a strategic communications manager, and an advising manager.[2] The five of us worked so well together primarily because we are a diverse group made up of two musicians, a history major, a language faculty member, and a social scientist: we are the liberal arts in action. Our larger team, the core leadership team, included all department heads and a few additional faculty members with specific, relevant roles or expertise. Before our first meeting, I outlined a set of core values to guide our work as follows:

The Core Leadership Team will protect the following core values:

- the broader public health
- the safety and well-being of students, staff, and faculty
- the provision of a quality liberal arts experience for all students
- we will lead with integrity, patience, and grace.

Having those values as an anchor allowed us to operate through the most challenging weeks any of us had ever experienced. We checked all major decisions against our values and used them to determine when to push back against mandates that we felt conflicted with our values. It's important to note that we lived by an unarticulated set of values before the crisis (excepting the focus on public health). This led me to note on LinkedIn, in the first of a series of leadership lessons, that "If you are not clear about your values under normal circumstances, you will not have them as an anchor in crisis. Responding to a crisis without values is nothing more than reacting; reacting is not leadership."

I learned much from the failures and successes of those weeks and documented that experience online.[3]

Most of what my team and I learned during the first months of the crisis can be summed up as follows: your character is revealed by crisis. While we articulated many specific lessons about bureaucracy, the nature of crisis management, and the many things that made our work more difficult, the most important work in crisis leadership occurs well before a crisis happens. The foundation for good leadership cannot be constructed during such uncertainty; bad hires will hurt you in a crisis in ways that you cannot imagine during routine times; and arrogance will severely limit your effectiveness. We have experienced the effects of bad leadership at every level during COVID-19, from our own institution to the federal government and every level in between. For those interested in administration, I would urge you to learn how to lead effectively during routine times. Make an effort to invest in your professional development and your team before crisis hits and know why you are in leadership so that you have a reason to press through challenges.

In order to respond effectively to the many challenges presented by COVID-19, we worked well beyond our typical duties. For example, my team and I measured classrooms to determine safe capacity limits. We identified outdoor instructional spaces when the university leadership decided not to pursue those options and set up a reservation system for outdoor space. Preserving and expanding access to instruction allowed our faculty to focus on course delivery techniques. We made mistakes and had to own them publicly. For example, in a desperate attempt to provide some normalcy for students and faculty, we scheduled an outdoor festival for late October. Within days of making the announcement, COVID-19 cases began to surge in our area. We made the difficult decision to cancel the event and acknowledge that scheduling it was not a good idea. Throughout the crisis, we held open sessions for faculty and staff to ask questions and share concerns. Frequently, we did not have the answers and did not pretend otherwise. But we took their concerns and questions seriously and kept communication open. Of all of our efforts, the open communication was most appreciated and probably most meaningful. A lot of what we did to live out our values went unseen, but the decision not to hide from our challenges and the many ways in which we solved problems for faculty reinforced that we were living our values, which gave us the credibility to ask our faculty and staff to do the important and hard work required to deliver effective instruction in the most challenging of circumstances.

Across campus in nearly every area, my colleagues rose to the challenge and served our students admirably. I am proud of my team, the faculty and staff in liberal arts and beyond, and our students, many of whom struggle in ordinary circumstances. Yet, I decided to leave. Knowing when it is time to say yes to an opportunity is a challenge. Although I built a strong network at MTSU, working with a lot of people I genuinely like, and for a provost I like and respect, the decision to leave still makes sense professionally and personally. I joined the University of Tulsa (TU) as dean of the Kendall College of Arts and Sciences just as they implemented a new strategic plan. This new opportunity allows me to leave MTSU with a strong foundation for success and join TU at a pivotal moment. My enthusiasm for the value of the liberal arts and the many skills I have gained in my time at MTSU will sustain me in my work with a new team. I am confident the experience I bring to my new institution has been well-tested by my time at MTSU and, moreover, that the move to a different type of institution will provide growth opportunities for me as well.

Many years ago, while working as a helper in an auto body shop, I was washing a car outside in the snow and had an epiphany: as a woman, I would never get ahead without an education. The life ahead of me was one of unrelenting struggle. Although I did have my GED (General Education Development Test) at that point, I knew it was not enough. Fortunately, my family lived in a town that had a community college and they let me come home to start over. It took six years and three institutions before I ended up in Jack Turner's classroom at MTSU where my life was changed. Many faculty members, almost all of them in liberal arts courses, influenced and inspired me along the way. They encouraged my curiosity and gave me the confidence to continue. My goal when I became a faculty member was to repay what had been given to me.

As an administrator, I am able to magnify the effects of that commitment by helping faculty succeed. When I recognized the existential threat facing the liberal arts, I decided that I could not sit by comfortably in my tenured position while access to a quality liberal arts education was undermined for future students. I found my purpose in championing the liberal arts as valuable, both as a means to a fulfilling career and the foundation of a meaningful life. It seems simplistic to say that I never imagined this career trajectory, but it is true. I had no plan, and I have no grand plans beyond doing my best in the place I find myself, treating people well, and trying to do the right thing. Those things alone would make an excellent legacy. If anything else stands the test of time, I will consider myself fortunate indeed.

Notes

[1] I cannot overstate the importance of shedding biases you might have against leadership studies. There are excellent resources in the field (there is also a lot of fluff, of course). *Dare to Lead* by Brené Brown; *Multipliers* by Liz Wiseman; *Good to Great* by Jim Collins are a few of my favorites.

[2] To Brad Baumgardner, Matthew Hibdon, Leah Lyons, and H. Stephen Smith: thank you! I'm proud of our work together and grateful for your friendship.

[3] LinkedIn. 2021. www.linkedin.com/in/kkpetersen

Leadership Preparation

Ten

How to be a Dean? Prepare for a Pandemic

Sheryl I. Fontaine

California State University, Fullerton

Abstract

On the morning of March 17th, as I prepared to be a virtual dean during a global pandemic, my reflex was to grab the work that I knew would need doing. What I hadn't considered during those anxious hours of preparation for abandoning campus, was that the preparation for that departure had begun the day that I had become the dean of the college. I had entered the office with a promise to myself that we would be present for and in one another's work and would share a set of values strong enough to undergird every decision we made alone or together, every inquiry we initiated, and every plan we announced. In this brief reflection, I will consider how the strength of our shared knowledge and collective vision was woven into place long before we walked out of our office doors for the last time and has been solidly beneath us during this most remarkable year.

Keywords: administrative structures, California State University, citizenship, community engagement, COVID-19, decentralized authority, empathy, English, feminist-informed administration, global awareness, isolation, minority-serving public university, pandemic, part-time faculty, social justice, virtual instruction, writing program administration, Zoom

***

Pulling into the line of cars leaving the parking lot, I glanced down at the red tapestry book bag in the passenger seat, so loaded with papers and files that I hadn't been able to close the zipper. Had I packed everything I would need, I wondered, as I turned left onto Nutwood Avenue and then entered the freeway ramp? When would the California stay-at-home order end? Had I remembered to pack the files that had to be reviewed? Were the right documents waiting for me in the Cloud?

Eight years ago, when I was appointed dean for the College of Humanities and Social Sciences, a large, interdisciplinary college at a very large minority-serving public university, I had already spent decades building and directing peer tutoring centers and administering writing programs. My research on writing program administration was informed by what I considered to be the best feminist, process, and social cognitive thinkers and writers of the time. I had written conferences papers, articles, and book chapters that both analyzed changes in administrative structures and described the way these structures looked in the centers and programs that I directed. In fact, my own professional interest in the value that feminist administrative structures can hold for the future of higher education and the growth of an increasingly diverse professoriate had been central to my decision to apply for the position of dean.

But on the day in March 2020 when we hastily prepared to leave the campus, and in many of the days that would immediately follow, I would not be harking back to the comfort that those years of experience should have provided.

Shuttling between dark humor and reassuring optimism, everyone in the dean's office spent much of that last day on campus scrambling to collect things to take home, looking through digital and paper files, uploading and downloading documents as we made preparations to "stay-at-home." With the advantage of hindsight, what I can see now, but didn't recognize on that day ten months ago, was that the preparation for our departure from campus had actually begun years prior.

Almost since the first day I became dean, I started the morning with an office walkabout, stopping by the individual offices of Jessica, Paul, and Pat: the associate dean of students, the associate dean of faculty and staff, and the budget manager. Leaning against each office door or, if invited, sitting in a guest chair, I'd simply ask, "So, what's happening?" It never ceased to amaze me how much work from the previous day had percolated into the hours after 5 p.m.: emails, data, message replies, and phone calls. Some mornings these conversations were brief, and I'd be back at my desk or off to my first meeting across campus in half an hour. But more often than not, much of the work of the day was shaped by these three unstructured conversations that spilled into one another, led to a phone call or an email, or generated a series of meeting makers. Conversations inevitably reached across offices, and Paul and I would ask Jessica to join us, or the three of us would cluster in Pat's office.

These unstructured, quotidian conversations that lent focus to our daily work, were syncopated against scheduled weekly, two-hour meetings among the four of us. Structured around agenda topics that emerged from our respective conversations and meetings in the college and throughout the university, we gathered our individual experiences into the strength of shared knowledge. We wrestled with problems whose solutions could be found in our collective effort.

Very soon after we had landed in isolation, with real and electronic miles between and among us, I was grateful for the strength of our collective spirit and the shared knowledge and perspectives that we had created. In those first weeks, my inbox and meeting schedule burst with questions and decisions around how to support a college of 10,000 students and 500 faculty on a campus of 41,000 students and 2000 faculty as each was expected to move their learning and teaching from the classroom to the computer within a matter of days. At the same time, Jessica was bombarded with questions from students about access and support and from faculty about course redesign; Paul received endless requests from frustrated and frightened faculty and staff and impossible demands from well-intended department chairs; and Pat valiantly engaged in realigning an already-overstretched college budget. But each of the decisions we made or directions we set in those early days of our COVID-19 isolation, was done with the sureness of the collaborated experience and knowledge we had been steadily creating long before this moment. The decisions that each of us had to make in our isolation was informed by what we had come to know from one another about ways that the pieces of our puzzle fit together.

In the time before our isolation, each week began with the ubiquitously familiar "Monday morning staff meeting." Our meeting included Paul, Jessica, and Pat, and all of our direct reports: Cindy, Joanna, Brittney, Connie, Jaycee, Emilia, Mari. Though the conference room has two entrances, we entered through our small, convenience kitchen, where we would collect our mugs of coffee, or cups of steaming tea, or environmentally friendly goblets of pastel-colored power drinks. The conversation we had as we took our seats around the table was likely very similar to that of Monday morning staff meetings everywhere: "How many soccer games did you attend?" "Did you see that new film?" "Were you able to get to the beach like you had planned?"

It took me a few months to shift the meeting itself away from being like so many Monday morning staff meetings, what I will call the "reporting for duty" meeting. At these meetings, one by one, each person reports whatever they think will assure or impress whomever is sitting at the head of the table. And as they await their turns to speak, everyone else daydreams, reads email, or make notes about what they will say when it's their turn. No one really listens to anyone else. And the meeting usually ends just about the time that everyone has reported in.

My goal was to structure this staff meeting so that it parallels the way the office works—individuals working alone but in concert with one another and in relation to the whole. I had created a similar meeting design for the English Department Writing Center. The tutors had created a set of "guilds" (a term the English majors used to replace "committee") into which the work of the center could be distributed. The tutors then selected one guild in which they would serve—workshop planning, advertising, classroom support, tutoring best practices, scheduling—and our weekly staff meetings were structured around the guild reports. By the end of each meeting, the thoughts, concerns, and suggestions of individual tutors had been voiced in the context of the work of each guild, and each guild's contribution to the management of the center and to the shared principles of peer tutoring.

To create a similar sense of connection across individuals and offices and in the context of shared goals, I organized the conversation for our dean's office staff meeting around topics that would most naturally involve multiple people and multiple areas of the office.

On the topic of faculty contracts and schedules: Cindy and Joanna describe the new technology and the challenges they face when creating hundreds of part-time faculty contracts. Jessica shares the semester-start enrollment analysis and identifies how many and which of the thousands of classes across the college our students seem to be avoiding. Pat reminds us how much each of our part-time faculty positions is underfunded by the campus budget model.

On the topic of time to degree: Connie and Britney describe the mandatory campus-wide advising meeting where they were instructed to encourage all students to enroll in 30 units each academic year. Mari outlines the new branding guidelines coming from Strategic Communications that focus attention on alumni career success. Jaycee worries aloud about the small number of students enrolling in the GE (general education) study abroad trip to Thailand that, if cancelled, would prevent three students from graduating.

At the weekly staff meetings, like the weekly meeting with Pat, Paul, Jessica, we brought to the room the information and knowledge gathered from our own respective meetings in and around campus, from the work that we were doing in our offices and with our closest colleagues And, rather than only four contributors to the growing collection of relevant experiences and perspectives, the staff meetings have eleven contributors. Through this co-created prism of information, we consider questions like whether or not to make last-minute course cancellations or additions, or how to understand the success and failures around our college four-year graduation targets.

As I write this essay, the office is watching enrollments for the upcoming spring semester, our second fully virtual semester. At the same time, we are reviewing the schedules that departments have drafted for the following fall semester when we hope that the spread of the virus will have adequately diminished so that the chancellor of the 23 campus California State University system can keep his promise for instruction to be largely in-person. So, while this moment in history may be unprecedented, the topics we face in the college have a familiar ring: How many course sections should be scheduled (when classes are in unbounded virtual spaces)? How can we predict which sections will fill (when students' lives have been so dramatically upended)? How can we close opportunity gaps (that have stubbornly persisted and even grown with increased availability of pass/fail)? How do we identify and manage best teaching practices (as we consider the impact of virtual instruction on our students and our faculty)?

Considering these questions, I am grateful now for every Monday morning that the staff had gathered around the laminated conference table and for each time one of us interrupted the other with an unconsidered perspective, added some recently received data, or offered up a cautionary story from experience. For even though, today, we can only see one another as illusory collections of pixels on a screen, Cindy and Joanna still experience the challenges of writing hundreds of contracts in light of what they learned from Jessica about low-enrolled classes and from Pat about budgeting perils when classes are added or deleted. We all consider students' imperfect progress toward four-year degrees in light of a campus message that sometimes denies the heterogeneous demographic of our students and the emotional and labor costs of such a large campus.

Reflecting on my own experience as a faculty member, I realize that it was not until I became the chair of the English Department that I knew much—or cared much—about the implications of being part of a college. Of course, I had known the other departments existed, but it wasn't until I attended my first meeting as a department chair that I truly appreciated the academic breadth of our college. The former dean hosted the chairs' meeting in a conference room where long tables had been arranged in a large square, with enough seating for every department and program chair. Stepping into that room and taking my seat, I came face to face with the faculty who were responsible for managing nineteen departments and forty-degree programs that represent the most essential academic disciplines in higher education and form much of our university general education program. These departments include some of the largest and smallest ones on campus; many that were foundational to the university; three that are fully interdisciplinary; and several that originated in the spirit of activism and change.

It is a point of pride for faculty members that their department identities and allegiances are strong and that the connections they make with their students endure well beyond graduation. To grow those connections in the English department, I had established an alumni event, crafted a section on our website devoted to "what to do with an English degree," and conducted an extensive survey of alumni that traced the circuitous route from degree and to career. But joining the college leadership team as a department chair, I realized that I, like most faculty, had not extended that same pride of identity and allegiance to the college.

Without a sense of the *College* of Humanities and Social Sciences, we cannot call attention to the heart of the campus, the locus of the disciplines most historically significant to all of higher education and most responsible for the habits of mind and personal values that make every graduate a more culturally engaged, historically-informed citizen and a more intellectually prepared and empathetically responsive employee. Without a sense of *college*, departments cannot grow their own identities in the fertile soil of a broad-based scholarly and academic tradition that is centuries old.

Several years after being appointed chair of the English Department, I sat at my laptop writing a letter of intent for the position of dean of the college and explained to the search committee that one of my goals would be to create a college identity, one that was far more historically rich and intellectually significant than simply being "the largest college on campus."

During my second year as dean, I was ready to find a starting place for establishing a much-needed college identity. I challenged the department chairs to select values that would represent a shared vision across the college. Today, far from campus, I hold in my mind's eye the image of the mid-century modern Humanities and Social Sciences building after dark, when a spotlight illuminates the honeycombed concrete that encloses the multi-floor balcony from which three twenty-five-foot-long banners hang. Side by side, the banners announce to the campus our college values: social justice, global awareness, community engagement. On each banner is also the face of one of three students selected to be the "Faces of HSS" (Humanities and Social Sciences) looking out over the campus and stalwartly awaiting our return. The process of selecting these values was not quick or easy for the nineteen department chairs. But the result that the discussion had on the relationship among the departments and the suitability of the chairs' choice of values became immediately apparent as we used social justice, global awareness, and community engagement to inform the topics we selected for the HSS Interdisciplinary Lecture series; decisions for collegewide strategic budgeting, philanthropic efforts, curricular and co-curricular opportunities; and even the narrative reflections that individual faculty members write for their promotion and tenure files.

The college pledge to social justice has taken on particular significance as the nation faces abhorrent acts of racial injustice, brutality, and violence perpetrated in the past several months, starting in late May 2020. At a Zoom meeting with the group of chairs who serve on the College Budget Committee, we talked about what it would mean to remove the racial inequities endemic to college processes and policies. Doing so would necessitate a redistribution of the baseline budget that is currently calculated in relation to full-time faculty positions, a re-evaluation of age-old scheduling practices that reward over enrollment, and a close look at faculty workload that ignores the inequities of the cultural tax—the additional but commonly unrewarded work of mentoring, advising, and committee participation that falls on the shoulders of our BIPOC (Black, Indigenous People of Color) faculty. With awareness that these changes will reduce resources for some departments, the committee readily agreed with the plan and asked that it be presented to the entire group of college chairs. I am confident that the support from the Budget Committee will be echoed by their colleagues when we present to them a plan built on funding formulas that advantage service-heavy workloads, college commitments to diversity and inclusion, and growth ahead of funding.

Due to nothing other than unlucky timing, the university is also in the throes of readying a campus-wide Ethnic Studies requirement that was recently legislated for the entire California State University system. Few things resonate more fully through our entire college than major changes in general education, and this one, in particular, will impact departments in both the humanities and social sciences and the general education categories that each steward. While our campus has a long and proud tradition that places the curriculum squarely in the hands of the faculty, I was unsure how this privilege and responsibility would be accepted by our faculty at a moment when they are physically absent from one another and experiencing significant personal and professional challenges from the pandemic. With pride, I have watched the college chairs arrange dozens of meetings via Zoom and conversations via email in order to design a united college position that celebrates this exciting sea change for African American Studies, Asian American Studies, and Chicano/Chicano Studies and graciously recognizes the impact the change will have for many of their own course offerings and enrollment targets. Together, the chairs are finding their way toward a principled argument that staunchly celebrates the importance of the new Ethnic Studies requirement for all students while also sharing the compromises that ensue. And when the discussion goes to the academic senate later this month, their case will be framed in the college identity that we have worked diligently to establish, a collective recognition that a balanced and thorough general education program benefits all students, a reminder to the campus of the importance that courses in the humanities and social sciences hold for every well-rounded undergraduate degree.

On the morning of March 17th 2020, as I prepared to be a virtual dean during a global pandemic, my reflex was to grab the work that I knew would need doing. What I hadn't considered during those anxious hours of preparation for abandoning campus, was that the preparation for that departure had begun the day that I had become the dean of the college. On that day, I entered the office with the same promise to myself that I had made in the writing center and the writing program, a promise to lead so that we in the college would be present for and in one another's work and would share values strong enough to undergird every decision we made alone or together, every inquiry we initiated, and every plan we announced. The books and papers I grabbed before leaving campus in March certainly have allowed my work to move forward this year, but the resilient warp and weft of our shared knowledge and collective vision has been solidly beneath us during this most remarkable year and was woven into place long before we walked out of our office doors for the last time.

I am grateful to have been invited to reflect on being a dean. Had the editors sent this invitation a year and a half ago, my reflections would still have coalesced around the significance that structures of feminist-informed administration and its commitment to decentralized authority and collaboration have had for me and for the college. However, receiving the invitation during a pandemic, while working from the isolation of home, miles from colleagues or campus, I have appreciably raised the measure of significance that these administrative structures hold. That they served me well during 20 years of administering writing centers and writing programs was certainly an important measure of their value. That they have served the college so well during this most unparalleled and unprecedented year is an even greater indication of their meaning.

Like colleges and universities around the globe, our university is beginning preparations for a return to campus that will be much slower and more wary than our departure. This won't be a move back to where we were, but a move forward, informed by where we have been. How has the work we do together been changed after a year of human distancing, technologically-confined communication, and daily uncertainty? What happens when conversations are both more intentional and more precious? Have we become better listeners as access to physical cues has decreased and the presence of verbal cues moderated through Wi-Fi has increased? What is the result when our inclination to collaborate has not diminished, but our access to one another has?

I look forward to the day when I can, once again, climb the stairs to the second floor of the Humanities and Social Sciences building, make my way to my corner office, place my red tapestry bag on the credenza behind my desk, and pause to listen to the familiar and unmodulated voices of colleagues outside my door. I am guardedly excited to learn how the viral fires of this year have tempered the principles and values that I so purposefully cultivated, that each of us carried from campus, and that piloted us through every day, week, and month since March. And I am eager to learn what we, together, will bring into the future of our college and our university.

Eleven

A Dean's Letter to a Friend
Considering a Dean Posting

Emily A. Haddad

University of Maine

Abstract

In the form of a letter to a colleague, this essay narrates the author's route into academic administration while also caring for a family and managing other professional roles. With experience as associate dean at one flagship research university and dean at another, the author describes the rewards and challenges of collaborative administrative work in the service of public higher education.

Keywords: academic administration, advising, budget deficit, Comparative Literature, English, department chair, graduate coordinator, Harvard University, leadership, pandemic, scholarship, student government experience, University of South Dakota, University of Maine

***

Dear Whitney,

Thank you for calling to catch up during your sabbatical. The dean posting we talked about just came out, and I hope you will apply. Your call—and a coincidental invitation to submit an essay (this letter!) about my trajectory into my current position—have got me thinking about how I ended up as dean and why I have stayed in the role.

 Although you and I have been friends since high school, I don't think we have ever talked about how I started in academic administration. Growing up in a college town, daughter of a professor and a writer/artist/editor, I have always had an intuitive feeling for the values and rhythms of academia. As you know, I didn't assume that from childhood that I would be an academic myself—but I'm sure you were not surprised to see me follow that path. It wasn't the path of least resistance, though. I knew when I started graduate school that a tenure-track job with a comparative literature PhD would be a huge stroke of luck, not something to count on. As it turned out, I was one of the lucky few to receive a tenure-track offer.

The turn to administration came soon after. It was a misunderstanding, actually. I was heading into my second year as a new assistant professor of English at the University of South Dakota (USD), with a much-appreciated 2-2 teaching load. I heard my department chair, Susan Wolfe, say that she expected teaching loads to increase. USD was very lightly unionized, I was very inexperienced, and I did not feel I could object if this change were made. Shortly afterwards, she asked me to become coordinator for the department's MA and PhD programs. I agreed, thinking that this would protect me from an increased teaching load. I realized pretty soon that the talk about an increased load was just talk, but by then it seemed too late, too awkward to back out. Also—and this won't surprise you, knowing me—I was interested in making the program work better.

This graduate coordinator role, along with getting to know the graduate students, turned out to be truly satisfying.[1] My first advising appointment, with an incoming doctoral student, was a disaster because there was no graduate student handbook or other written materials beyond what was in the catalog. My colleagues had devised the doctoral program with considerable ingenuity and great dedication. My task was to operationalize it. Eventually I pushed to simplify it as well, and to create tighter connections between the various stages, so that students would move in a more natural way from coursework to exams, to an approved prospectus, to a defense and a degree. The master's program needed similar work. Both programs recruited on the "if we build it they will come" model. As you might imagine, the results were erratic. So, more targeted and effective recruiting became another top project. I knew from my student government involvement at Harvard that USD teaching assistants were earning about half of what a Harvard graduate student earned, for considerably more work. Addressing that issue was part of the recruitment plan, and also a moral imperative. Fortunately, Susan and her successor, Brian Bedard, were supportive of these efforts, if somewhat bemused and occasionally annoyed by the ferocity with which I pursued them.

Thinking back, my graduate student government experience was key preparation for this first "real" administrative role. Although Harvard was not new to me when I went there for graduate school, I don't think that when you and I were undergraduates at Harvard either of us had much sense of the institution as such. My recollection is that we knew our own programs and had some idea about contiguous areas (Near Eastern Languages and Cultures, and English for me; History and the Medical School for you). We didn't know or care about much beyond that, and we did not have any idea of how the various pieces of Harvard, or any other research university, actually fit together. Our experience growing up across the street from Smith College might have helped a little, but not much, even for me as a faculty brat. Graduate Student Council (GSC) was really the first opportunity I had to gain that insight. I had a chance to meet and work collaboratively with fellow students from a huge diversity of fields. I also took advantage of the access provided to administrators (Administrative Dean Margot Gill particularly) and to the faculty meetings of the Graduate School of Arts and Sciences, which officers of the GSC were permitted to attend as observers. I remember Dean Jeremy Knowles rising from his seat to impress upon colleagues that they must address the looming budget deficit, a topic that would not otherwise have reached my consciousness. Surely, I had no idea then how much of my future career would be spent on looming budget deficits!

GSC also gave me my first opportunity to effect positive change at my institution. With a couple of other officers, I worked to establish a travel grant program for graduate students to attend conferences, paid for by the fees already charged to each graduate student. I just looked at the GSC website and saw that a version of this program still exists 25 years later. That's gratifying, but the more formative aspect of the experience for me was really the collaboration. Like your field, scholarship in mine tends to be solitary. My previous leadership experiences were as a counselor at summer camp—you will relate to that too, I know. Those experiences were both highly collaborative and closely focused on specific projects. GSC work was satisfying in many of the same ways, ways that my scholarly work and teaching were not, much as I loved them for other reasons.

Having the twins in my last year of graduate school created a different set of management challenges. John was working full-time managing large renovation projects for a Boston contractor, I was fighting a losing battle with sleep deprivation while nursing two babies after a physically exhausting pregnancy, and the babies took all I had, despite my mother helping out for much of their first months. Anything not absolutely necessary receded. You probably noticed that I was not much in touch with you during that period. Anyway, I finished the dissertation, interviewed for jobs, got one, and we moved to Vermillion, SD. The boys were about 16 months old. While John was primarily responsible for them during the day, caring for two toddlers with strong opinions did not leave either of us much time to spare. In retrospect, taking the graduate coordinator job in my second year on the tenure track was evidence that, for the first time in a couple of years, I could envision doing something more than the bare minimum required to stay afloat.

The graduate coordinator role provided its own insights into my new institution. I began working together with colleagues in a way reminiscent of the GSC collaboration—organizing a graduate student research exposition with a faculty member from another college, for example. The graduate coordinator also functioned as associate chair, which meant involvement in a range of decisions from assignment of TAs (teaching assistants) to carpet selection for the department office. During this time, I also became closely involved in USD's honors program, which opened more collaborative opportunities, especially with a colleague in History, Kurt Hackemer, whose administrative path would zigzag across mine over the next decade. I did occasionally think about becoming chair but imagined it as an option for later. Our third son arrived on his brothers' first day of kindergarten, and I felt I had plenty to do without chairing a department.

A chair search was announced by the college's new-ish dean when our youngest was still a toddler. I applied with mixed feelings. I had, as just noted, plenty to do already. My first book, based on my dissertation, had been published, and I was well into a second long project. I was also eagerly anticipating my first-ever (and it turns out, my one-and-only) sabbatical the next fall. Finally, I was junior for the role, just a couple of years post tenure, and I knew at least one senior colleague would also apply. That's awkward in any department, but it's particularly awkward in a town that is about 3 miles across, where the faculty are all each other's neighbors. Nudging me to apply was my confidence that at least some of my colleagues believed that I was the person for the job, and also the signals from the dean's office that if there were not a legitimately competitive search, an external hire would be pursued instead. I was proud of what my department had accomplished. Viewed objectively, though, this chair job did not seem like a great catch on the national market for English Department chairs, especially given the University of South Dakota's isolated location. I was leery of the results of an external search. Would we get a "seagull administrator," flying in to poop on everything and then leaving us with the mess? Would we have a complacent chair, who wouldn't see our potential? I submitted my application.

The search was genuinely competitive, with a very close vote in the department and some hard feelings when I was announced as the next chair. The first year was, to use one of the dean's favorite terms, "bumpy." I started in January, which meant that one of my very first tasks was to write the contractually mandated annual evaluation for every member of the department. More hard feelings. Four months in, I got my cancer diagnosis, which meant taking several months off for surgery and recovery. My academic accomplishments for that year were minimal. Still, some of the housekeeping measures had a positive effect on morale. There was a clean coat of paint over the aging off-yellow in the corridors. An empty TA office, temporarily designated as a technology morgue, prompted faculty members to deaccession a huge pile of non-functional computers and peripherals, leaving everyone with a little less clutter in their offices. The dean agreed to renovate and furnish a decrepit oversized office upstairs so that the department would have a professional-looking meeting space, and then the director of the campus art gallery lent some paintings for the walls. Working in a respectable space makes people feel respected. My colleagues deserved that, and it felt good to be able to give it to them.

As you know, I chaired the English Department for about six years, and was promoted to professor about half way through. These years included the Great Recession after the 2008 crash, but they were otherwise good years for the university. The department did pretty well. I continued to teach at least one course each semester, and I was still publishing, though much more slowly than I would have without the administrative responsibilities. Having it all (family, teaching, scholarship, administration) was a lot. I think I remember falling asleep on the living room floor when you visited. That would have been common.

At that time, USD appointed chairs to serve at the pleasure of the dean, without set terms. The longest-serving chair in the college had been in the job 14 years when I joined the Chairs' Council. He is still chair now, over 30 years from when he started. So, I wasn't making any definite assumptions about how long I would serve. As far as I could tell, my colleagues weren't either. In short, chairing seemed as if it could become a long plateau. I continued to wrestle with whether Vermillion was where I wanted to be; the twins were becoming tweens and then teens; and my mother was showing the first mystifying signs of the Parkinson's that would ultimately kill her. Clarity of direction felt impossible to achieve. Mostly I was too busy and too tired.

Given all this, an opening for associate dean felt like a solution to a problem that I hadn't fully formulated. I could park in the same parking lot, avoid the bigger questions about where to be, and still have a new job. As chair of a large department, I had generated much of the business that the associate dean had to deal with, so I had a reasonably good idea of what the job entailed. I would be replacing Kurt, my historian colleague, who was about to become associate provost, so I knew I would have his help in learning what I didn't know. I told the dean I was interested, and that was pretty much that. I left the department in good hands and moved from Dakota Hall to the Arts and Sciences building on the other side of the parking lot.

This proved a much smoother transition than becoming chair. Still, there were some surprises. Although I knew the other chairs pretty well, I didn't know their departments. By default, I assumed that their departments worked like the English Department. That was fair enough for the other larger, doctoral-granting departments, but it was a complete misunderstanding of the smaller ones. I remember printing out the sociology course schedule and thinking I must have left a page in the printer—but no, there just weren't very many sociology classes. I couldn't continue to assume that what worked for a big department that delivered programs from the remedial to the doctoral would be relevant to all.

There were two other significant differences. First, as associate dean, I had to operate entirely by persuasion. The position was outside the college's chain of command. Like all the department chairs, I reported to the dean. Nobody reported to me, though. When I was department chair, I had resorted to "I'm telling you you have to do this" very rarely, but that option lent me authority even when I didn't use it. As associate dean, it wasn't there.

Second, the role required shifting several key relationships from occasional interaction to daily collaboration. Unlike the more project-focused collaborations that had been meaningful to me before, these were structurally essential to my job. For instance, being associate dean for academics meant co-leading with the associate dean for administration. The dean, Matthew Moen, was an outstanding fundraiser who was often away from the office and had to trust us to manage in his absence. The other associate dean and I shared a fondness for cats and a capacity for hard work, and had different perspectives on many other topics. The complementary working relationship we developed served the college well and is something I will always be proud of. Another key relationship was with the Advising Center director and staff. I had to be able to fill in as an advisor during summer registration days for new students, but also be the decision-maker when a student appealed a suspension or a grade. Understanding the advising operation well was necessary for my own effectiveness as associate dean. I continue to be grateful for the staff members who had the patience to teach me what I didn't know.

The biggest institutional change during the time I served as associate dean was the implementation of responsibility center management (RCM) as the university's budget model. As dean, Matt made the decisions for the college, but the associate deans also participated in all the meetings with the financial staff who were actually creating USD's version of the RCM model. The planning was detailed and intensive. Again, it showed me what I didn't know about things I had thought I understood. It prompted us all to address questions that would have been irrelevant in the modified incremental budgeting model we had been using for years. Which departments made money? Which ones had to be subsidized? Did the subsidies match our academic values? How could we sustain open communication about college finances without inadvertently setting departments against each other?

When I was three years in, Matt asked me about applying for the dean position at his former institution, the University of Maine. I had seen the posting during my nightly scroll through open administrative jobs on the *InsideHigherEd* website, but the scrolling wasn't associated with any actual intention of applying for any job. Matt agreed with me that this particular job was probably out of my league. I had a solid scholarly record but not a lengthy one. Despite his efforts to encourage me over the years, I had not succeeded in finding time to improve my publication rate. He believed that the University of Maine would want to hire a top-flight scholar. Nonetheless, he made the point that if I wanted to get back to New England (did I? was that an actionable goal?) I should consider applying anyway.

I pondered. From a family perspective, the opening was well-timed. The twins were in their senior year in high school and they both wanted to leave South Dakota for college. They would not be a limiting factor in any decision to move. Their younger brother was in seventh grade and moveable. Although the twins had each found a path through Vermillion High School, their experiences there didn't inspire me to want to send a third child—it was okay, but not great. John said he was willing to move if a job in Maine worked out. So I applied.

I got the job, as you know. It was a slow search process, and I assumed at each stage that I hadn't made the cut. When the UMaine provost actually called with the offer, though, it wasn't a huge surprise. The on-campus interview had gone well, I thought. Apart from the matter of the scholarly record, I had the kind of preparation you would expect for a position like that. Interviewing when you expect nothing and don't need a job is relatively low stress, and it was probably evident that I was enjoying myself. And I figured that if the number of publications were going to be a problem, I would have been cut before the campus visit.

The search committee chair, another dean, had done me the kindness of disclosing the salary range approved for the position. Mindful of the research about women not negotiating salary at the outset, I negotiated to the top of the range and accepted the position in early June. The posting had indicated a July 1 start, so I also had to negotiate a delay—there was just no way to move that fast. My decision to resign was not popular with my USD colleagues, and I didn't want to make matters worse by leaving a long list of projects not done. In the household arena, I was heading for Maine with our youngest and one of the twins, who was going to Harvard in the fall. John was staying behind to get the house ready to sell. The other twin, who was going to Beloit College, in Wisconsin, also stayed in South Dakota for the summer. Thanks to our dear friend Sally flying out from New Hampshire to help us pack, we were actually ready for the movers in mid-July. The next day, I loaded the mini-van, stacking the three cat crates in first, and drove east with the two boys. The cliché "haze of exhaustion" comes to mind. It's not easy to stay awake on a road as flat, straight, and empty as Route 20 across Iowa.

The UMaine job started July 28, with a three-year term. The main challenge of the first term was learning the ways of this new institution. UMaine's "vital statistics" resemble USD's—R-2 universities of similar size located in small towns in largely rural states, flagship campuses in state university systems that are oversized for the population served and resources available, etc. But their personalities, if you will, are different. As a first-time dean at a new university, I needed time to learn the players, policies, and histories. I felt slowed down by having to look up things I knew by heart at USD, and handicapped by ignorance of key facts not posted on websites (like, she used to be married to him? Really?). The college had been steadily losing full-time faculty for over a decade, thanks to an unwelcome tradition of annual budget cuts that prevented hiring as faculty members retired, resigned, or died. I had a clear mandate from the remaining faculty to turn that trend around, no matter what. Not easy. The tradition of cuts—or, more accurately, internal reallocations that enable the university to balance its budget—continued. In a glorious year without a cut, we made really good progress on hiring. In most other pre-pandemic years, we held steady or gained a little ground. On the one hand, I take pride in the against-the-odds achievement, and on the other hand it feels paltry.

On my first day, a member of the dean's office staff told me that no female dean had ever been reappointed. This is no longer true. I am now nearing the end of my third term. Faculty members I helped to hire very early on are starting to be tenured. It's a sweet reward. The grand purpose of the college—to advance and share knowledge—is real and worthy. The hard work of leading a college of arts and sciences within a research university still feels like a privilege. Overall, I've been well served by the 10-word administrative philosophy I adopted as a new associate dean at USD: (1) Eyes on the prize; (2) Chip away; (3) Feed the people. These have not been easy years, though. Even before Covid, the demands on my time and emotional resources at work were always more than I could fulfil. Family responsibilities continued too: the twins were increasingly independent but still needed my attention, my parents moved to a retirement community in town when I had been at UMaine for less than two years, our youngest was still with us at home, and when John's disabled younger brother was no longer able to live on his own, he came to Maine too, ending up in a nursing home just down the road. As you know, my mother's final years of dementia were especially hard.

The question now is less "why do you want to be a dean?" than "why do you want to stay a dean?" Deaning during a pandemic has been no fun. The volume of work is beyond what's possible. Planning for multiple contingencies takes time, over and over. The over-and-over part of it makes the whole thing less satisfying.

One of the program directors in my college, captain of an aircraft carrier in his former life, likes to talk about leadership in terms of Daniel Pink's idea that motivation is based on autonomy, mastery, and purpose. Purpose is still rock solid for me; I have no doubt that the college's mission merits the time and tears I continue to give it. The other two are shakier. In order to control spending, and perhaps also to prepare for the planned unified accreditation across all University of Maine System campuses, decisions that used to be made in the dean's office and rubber-stamped by a staff member in the provost's office now require four approvals above the provost. During the first semesters of the pandemic, routine activities, like theatre productions in the School of Performing Arts, had to be reviewed by the Emergency Operations Committee, the provost, and the president, based on a formal request that has to be personally submitted by me as dean. The result was less autonomy, with more time spent writing justifications and completing paperwork. There are new skills to be mastered too. I did not know before all of this what a "hierarchy of controls" was, or how to apply one for safety during a pandemic. I've learned, but it's still outside my comfort zone, and frankly also not very interesting to me. Tasks that I had mastered before, like overseeing the creation of the schedule of classes, had to be relearned because of different constraints: no more than 30 people present in person during a class meeting, new "instructional modes" to reflect the many approaches to remote teaching and learning, uncertainty about students' and faculty members' ability to be on campus and/or to arrange reliable internet connections at home. The list goes on. As the post-pandemic era continues to evolve month after month, I'm more and more aware of the likelihood that "post-pandemic" will be quite different from "pre-pandemic." "Post-pandemic" may demand many of the same adaptive moves as "pandemic" did, and may place many of the same pressures, even if not in exactly the same spots.

The same threats to autonomy and mastery that I have experienced are felt across the college's leadership team. Not coincidentally, there is also a new level of pastoral care expected and needed, but not yet mastered by me: #3, "Feed the people," is really tough when everyone is so isolated from one another. With our youngest now a junior at UMaine, purpose is really the key motivator (remember #1, "Eyes on the prize"). The occasional "thanks for that" helps too. The satisfaction of solving problems collaboratively is still compelling for me, and I deeply appreciate the people I have the honor to collaborate with in this role. Also: if I left the dean position, what would I do instead, and where would I do it? Thinking rationally about either of those questions mid-pandemic falls somewhere between unappealing and impossible.

You and I share the experience of public school, private university, and then a professional career in public higher education—perhaps initially by happenstance, but with growing and now profound conviction that a public university education is a societal good that is well worth tending with care. I hope that some of this story will be relevant to your decision about starting to apply for administrative jobs. Either way, good luck, and thanks for staying in touch.

Emily

Notes

[1] I don't need to tell you how meaningful these connections with students are—you know from your own experience as a faculty member at a similar public university. So my comments focus elsewhere. I acknowledge the students by dedicating these comments to the memory of two former graduate students who were especially dear: Sayaka Kanade (1980-2011) and Jason E. Murray, PhD (1973-2018).

Twelve

Advancing as a Faculty-Colleague's Academic Leader

Reginald A. Wilburn

Texas Christian University

Abstract

This essay serves as a reflection by a former associate dean on how the deanship provides a platform for a faculty member to support his colleagues in the humanities and social sciences through the enactment of transparent policies designed to promote equity. The deanship allows a faculty leader to practice the humanist principles of clear communication with empathy and a stalwart commitment to serving and supporting others through best practices of shared governance, inclusive excellence, and a respect for academic freedom. These commitments promote equal access for colleagues for a successful career and trajectory through interim-review to tenure and promotion to advanced professoriate ranks.

Keywords: antiracist pedagogy, associate dean, collaborative ethos, COVID-19, DEI, higher education, humility, leadership, shared governance, systemness, thrival, transparency

***

I came to academic leadership through a nontraditional pathway.[1] Not long after earning tenure, I applied for the internal position of associate dean for academic affairs in my college of liberal arts. I applied for this position having been nominated by three senior faculty members from my college, who also circulated a petition throughout the college seeking endorsements from my faculty colleagues. My nominators secured signatured endorsements of their nomination of me from more than 40 faculty members. I am grateful to my colleagues for this show of support, knowing faculty would not endorse me if they did not trust me to serve, support, and collaboratively lead alongside them in a shared effort to change the world one student at a time. I also know they would not have endorsed me if they did not have faith in my abilities to champion innovations in our curriculum, support faculty in and outside their classrooms, and lead efforts that would foster and advance diversity, equity, and inclusion initiatives consonant with the enduring power and beauty constitutive of our liberal arts disciplines.

I hold the above attributes from my profile as an administrative leader in high regard. I know and remain convinced just how much these attributes serve as highly valued navigational capital for senior faculty who transition from the faculty ranks to assume roles of administrative leadership in higher education. Navigational capital of this type proceeds from the strong constitutions of individuals whose actions prove true to their words, who instill faith and confidence in others, and whose entrepreneurial ideas inspire collaborative buy-in toward achieving the seemingly impossible. In today's COVID-19 climate and post-George Floyd and Breonna Taylor moment, such navigational capital is needed and highly prized, especially for administrative leaders whose commitments to providing students the premium education all deserve can benefit from the bodies of experiential knowledge it has been my good fortune to learn from and customize toward defining my personal theory of democratic leadership.

My personal theory of democratic leadership privileges a forthright and transparent style of collaborative engagement with all members of an institution's community. Additionally, my theory of leadership holds me accountable to embracing an unwavering commitment to shared governance and esteeming an inviolable regard for keeping Diversity Equity and Inclusion (DEI) excellence centrally organic to every task or initiative I undertake. I must also state that I consider no attribute of leadership greater to me than that of being integral to who I am as a person, the values I hold, the duties and responsibilities I am entrusted to discharge, and my relationships with others. Integrity is most important to me in terms of my leadership *ethos* because people typically find it difficult to follow those they do not trust or respect. James M. Kouzes and Barry Z. Posner's research supports this outlook on leadership. In *The Leadership Challenge*, Kouzes and Posner identify trustworthiness as the primary "personal trait, characteristic, and attribute" people in their survey ranked as the most important quality they admire in leaders.[2] Their findings align with some of the most valuable life lessons I learned about leadership from organic and traditional intellectuals in my family.

Familial Cultural Capital and Other Sources of Leadership Wisdom

I had no professional handbook at my disposal to guide me on best practices of administrative leadership at the point I accepted the offer to serve as associate dean for my college. In addition to reading the few articles given to me, I reflected on the leadership wisdom of key members in my family. This familial capital of cultural wealth has served me well throughout life, my teaching career, and the various billets of educational leadership I have held in service to humanity. Throughout the entirety of my life, I have known my mother to live her life authentically in an integral manner that echoes a phrase she has articulated far too many times to be forgotten by me. Specifically, she lives life authentically by letting her "yays be yay and [her] nays be nay." As I understand it, her vernacular expression means being true to herself consonant with the words she utters and the beliefs she espouses so no one can have any justifiable reason to perceive her as duplicitous or unworthy of their trust. I lead my life similarly, having learned early in life how valuable it is for people to know that, like my mother, I, too, "say what I mean and mean what I say." I find that this leadership trait is one worth protecting. Even in times when people disagree with me, I take comfort in knowing they can at least respect me for being true to my words and deeds.

My grandmother's imparted wisdom of "finishing like you start" offers another gem that has proven indispensable to me in leadership. Her wisdom especially reminds me of the virtue associated with being known as consistent in my way of doing things, treating people, and conducting business. Simply put, to finish like you start is to lead genuinely, consistently, and faithfully true to one's personality and dispositional approach to leadership. To switch up suddenly or periodically by uncharacteristically deviating from one's established mode of being and manner of conducting business is to create interpretive states that leaves one's colleagues confused about who one is as a professional. Leading in this manner is bound to give others reasonable cause to regard a leader of this dispositional type as unreliable, undependable, and untrustworthy. Indeed, different social contexts, protocols, and business affairs may require one to make certain attitudinal adjustments. Even then, however, one's overall professional character should not deviate from who one is within the sphere of leadership.

My maternal uncle's outlook on parenting constitutes a third valuable lesson on leadership I have learned from a family member. As an educator and administrative leader, I draw upon my uncle's metaphor of tightrope leadership not because I view students or colleagues as children. Rather, I find the implications of his precept for my administrative roles have more to do with how I am to understand myself and my leadership positionality with others. Keenly aware that humility and flexibility in higher education leadership will prove far more effective with colleagues than 'do as I say' styles of dictatorial management, I do my best to balance my style of collaboratively leading others as though I were walking a tightrope with balanced equilibrium. For my uncle, once parents notice they are being too strict or rigid, it is expedient for them to ease up by becoming more lax in their governance style. Conversely, when parents prove too lax, it may be necessary to firm up and find equilibrium by adopting a stricter governance style. In leadership, adopting a stricter governance style in such circumstances mitigates the possibility of being taken advantage of, dismissed, or ignored. Finding equilibrium through this flexibly adaptive style of governance can be achieved by metaphorically walking a tightrope of leadership. A goal should be to foster a spirit of collaborative buy-in as opposed to creating a climate where anything goes with little rhyme or reason.

Additional sources of leadership wisdom stem from lessons I have learned about administrative leadership from former and sitting presidents like Nancy Zimpher, Katherine Rowe, and Chris Howard. I credit Zimpher, a former president of SUNY (State University of New York) and the University of Wisconsin systems, for helping me to orient my approach to conceiving, developing, and implementing transformative change by thinking along synergistic matrices that create what she calls "systemness." Zimpher, coins this term to denote the process of "cultivating and engaging talent at every level" as a means for securing collaborative buy-in from institutional partners.[3] Entrepreneurial leaders in higher education create systemness by conceiving initiatives and executing them in networks that span the entirety of the institution while taking seriously the expertise of staff whose knowledge of student life within and beyond classroom experiences prove vital to the infrastructural oversight leaders are charged with exercising.

Zimpher's thoughts on systemness closely align with the leadership vision practiced at William & Mary by President Katherine Rowe and her executive team. President Rowe's cabinet operates from a collaborative *ethos* that privileges "holding the whole" of the institution. This collaborative approach to creating systemness means each member of the leadership team recognizes the individual goals for their respective units as intricately inter-dependent with those of their colleagues. When upheld by all members of a team, this leadership model strengthens systemness and matrix thinking up, down, and across the university based on individuals' inter-dependent concern for the work being done by colleagues who are tasked with managing the affairs of other institutional units.

From Chris Howard, president of Robert Morris University, I have learned the importance of supervising direct reports in a democratic manner that encourages them to "live within their 360-degree" experience of leadership development. This model resonates with my democratic leadership style because it honors direct reports' agential humanity. As a facilitating leader, I aim to learn from them how I might best support them to hold themselves personally accountable for setting and meeting individual goals or resetting and recalibrating them should they prove unsuccessful in doing so. Providing direct reports this autonomy of agential authority reconceptualizes how the workplace environment of leaders can function as a democratic professional space where professionals are empowered to discharge assigned responsibilities, meet individual leadership goals, and hold themselves accountable to standards of excellence.

Knowing One's Self-Defining Ground and Responsibilities
of Shared Governance Leadership

Thus far, I have emphasized the importance of being trustworthy, offered some home-grown principles of leadership, and shared lessons shared with me by three university presidents. Other things worth considering when transitioning from faculty ranks to administrative leadership include knowing and understanding the self in the fullness of one's personality type. Playwright, August Wilson, identifies this deep-seated knowledge of one's self and the cultural origins informing individuals' lives as a self-defining ground. Knowing and occupying this terrain of cultural truth proves vital for negotiating and navigating life in general and necessary for administrative leaders specifically. So much of effective leadership in academia depends on socially interacting with diverse individuals and publics as well as yours and their distinct temperaments and dispositions. I possess an outgoing personality, am known for speaking my mind resolutely in a style I would characterize as tempered assertiveness. In whatever setting I find myself situated, I can be trusted to speak my truths with candor without dehumanizing others. When attempting to inspire collaborative buy-in on matters where agreement with me may not be unanimous, I try as best I can to convey my ideas in a style that aims to paint the picture of a given scenario commensurate with my ideas and logic. If my ideas prove agreeable to a majority, I am satisfied that consensus has been won on the merits of group members' collaborative buy-in as opposed to me coercing them to follow my beliefs and opinions solely because I demanded they do so. Appealing to these styles of communication means I am able to relay my thoughts affirmatively yet with a spirit of respectful diplomacy that ensures my thoughts will be heard without dominating the space with an air of dictatorial authority. Learning and refining this style of collaborative-seeking discourse was probably one of the most formidable challenges I experienced throughout my first six to eight months as an associate dean. Its art can and must be achieved if administrative leaders are to have high-impact success in collaborative engagements with faculty and staff colleagues.

This style of speaking resolutely and with the skilled artistry and tenor of respectful diplomacy must be mastered since governance structures in higher education do not imitate models of leadership practiced within private industry or military organizations. Leadership in higher education differs from private industry and the military in that our sector places as premium upholding the highest principles of shared governance and democratic leadership. Shared governance must be upheld in higher education because colleges and universities belong to each of their multiple constituents differently and in different degrees. My understanding of this shared ownership of colleges and universities by their constituents benefits from ecclesiastical sentiments expressed by Bishop

Jonathan E. Alvarado, who declares, "The church is God's by ownership, the people's by membership, and the bishop's by stewardship." His declaration reminds me of the shared governance model endorsed in higher education. Bishop Alvarado's philosophy concerning the church's organizational structure recognizes the rights, privileges, freedoms, and responsibilities pertaining to its different constituents. No one entity within the church can be understood as having sole authority for governing the institution.

The same holds true in higher education. More than a buzzword or idealized concept, shared governance must be upheld in higher education if the leadership work of doing the university is to remain vitally relevant. It will prove highly valuable if new and first-time administrative leaders take some time to consult authoritative texts that adequately define and explain shared governance prior to assuming their roles. Leaders need to know and understand the concept as well as the rights and responsibilities pertaining to members within academia. I make this recommendation, remembering that while I had heard the term "shared governance" bandied about by colleagues from the time I became an assistant professor, I never really knew what it meant until I became an associate dean. I have since learned I was not an anomaly in this respect relative to my faculty colleagues.

Colleges and universities, not unlike churches, belong to each of their constituents differently. They belong to students, faculty, staff, administrative leaders, presidents, boards of trustees, and global publics in ways that are distinct from the members of each of these social groups. For instance, colleges and universities belong to students in ways that they never can, will, or should for staff, faculty, or others. To be truly effective, administrative leaders should possess a resolute understanding of the different ways institutions belong to each of their constituent members, especially if few or no one else does. More important, we need to know where the convergences and divergences along these axes of membership meet and separate.

Arguably, more than anyone else for whom colleges and universities belong, it is necessary that administrative leaders know what shared governance means, is, and is not. Shared governance, in its most basic meaning, denotes a collaborative system and style of leadership where members within different organizational units and infrastructural levels enjoy decision-making authority according to the span of operating control designated in their respective roles of oversight expertise. This model of shared leadership does not entitle members to a freedom that is misunderstood as synonymous with license. Nor does shared governance mean those possessing decision-making authority have no restrictions on the determinations or resolutions ascribed to their executive roles. Rather, shared governance in its most ennobled practice confers upon each of its members rights and responsibilities, checks and balances so no one individual, group, or entity feels entitled to enjoy monopolized control over any determinative resolution related to the functioning and "thrival" of the institution.[4] Unlike management styles typical of corporate environments, shared governance in higher education should and must work for and by the people colleges and universities exist for and for the public good as well.

Leading Collaboratively, Advocating for Higher Education, and Championing the Liberal Arts

Much of the work administrative leaders do involves inspiring transformative change in collaboration with faculty, staff, and students. Other responsibilities include managing initiatives and crises. These demands require mastering inter-personal dynamics grounded in a respect for shared governance. Administrative leaders cannot hope to prove successful in inspiring change or managing crises without having mastered principles of shared governance as a practice of interpersonal engagement. First, administrative leaders will have to make an ideological readjustment to their institutions, cognizant that while still a member of the faculty, they now hold a different type of allegiance to those evaluating them within their unit's reporting structure. For this reason, friendships among colleagues can, must, and will change.

This does not mean one's colleagues instantly become enemies, however. It does mean that given your elevated fiduciary responsibilities coupled with the time-bound confidences expected of the role, you will not be able to disclose everything you know. In both lateral and vertical directions, promoting trustworthiness in these roles is paramount. Additionally, leading with an empathetic ear and a collaborative spirit can prove indispensable to one's ongoing success in these roles. I also recommend getting out of the office and walking the map of the campus routinely. Walking the campus map of the university, I find, keeps me on the pulse of what is happening in the lives of the diverse constituents I serve. I have also found this practice as conducive to demystifying for others the work occurring within one's often siloed office. Most important, walking the map of the campus affords truly engaged academic leaders rich opportunities for blending with faculty, staff, and students. This brand of navigational capital is not to be under-estimated as it helps to solidify within the hearts and minds of those one serves that you are souled-out to knowing them, caring for them, championing their individual and collective causes, and advocating for them and their units when threats to our shared avocation and work sometimes seems daunting if not dispiriting.

I also believe effective administrative leaders champion academic freedom as well. Faculty enjoy the freedoms to teach, research, and disseminate to global publics innovative scholarship, ideas, and formulae borne from individuals' funds of intellectual expertise. Such freedoms deserve uncompromised protection and advocacy. Breaches to these sacred freedoms in academia potentially undermine life and the generating of ideas that sustain it by circumscribing limits of knowledge and social routes to belief, that can lead to a tyranny of hegemonic ideas by those who would wield such power to satisfy individual gain.

I might add necessity demands that now, more than ever, administrative leaders must possess a ready and compelling gospel concerning the importance and high return on investment of higher education overall. We also need compelling clapbacks that would effectively challenge what I see as a disciplinary assault on the liberal arts and maligning of the general education curriculum. There can be no better return on investment than the twenty-first-century transformative citizens we teach, serve, and support for the public good of global society into perpetuity. As for the education we provide, the work of colleges and universities proceeds from a strong foundation built on the bedrock that is the general education curriculum. This time-honored curriculum combining the *trivium* and *quadrivium* provides the enduring life skills and habits that likewise position today and tomorrow's students to innovate that which societies need, fill the voids that will make life better, and win the souls of nations where liberty and justice has yet to be perfected. I contend this gospel of the liberal arts must be preached in and out of season without ceasing and in conjunction with a message that never lets the world forget why higher education must always matter.

DEI Leadership and Managing Conflict

Still another area of governance worth mentioning concerns the role that DEI excellence should hold in one's leadership portfolio. I believe it should go without saying that DEI excellence should manifest as a centrally organic component of every administrative leader's approach to change-management leadership. By centrally organic, I mean placing intentional commitments to ensuring principles of DEI excellence are constitutive of every initiative undertaken by leaders and constituent-colleagues alike. Leading with this commitment actively in mind means DEI excellence is never trivialized such that it materializes as an *a la carte* component of one's leadership portfolio. In areas of thought leadership, iteration, and implementation of collaborative initiatives, leaders should be able to point to myriad high-impact outcomes that echo the talk of vocally supporting DEI efforts across the university. Supporting faculty members' antiracist pedagogies is one way we might think of advancing DEI efforts. Championing the need for educational training, revising unit policies, and actively participating in co-developing problem-solving procedures anchored in comprehensive understandings of white ignorance, white fragility, and the intersectional workings of oppression across marginalized individuals' multiple identity contingencies are other ways we might advance such efforts through our leadership.

Administrative leaders should not expect faculty, staff, and students to pursue training in these areas if they are not pursuing educational opportunities in these areas also. Particularly for those whose academic training is not anchored in area or cultural studies, I should think administrative leaders would crave continuous and ongoing training in DEI principles. Attending sessions at deans' conferences, immersing themselves in the literature alongside others, and engaging in the cultures of marginalized communities often help to demystify the privileges, entitlements, and blind spots all of us hold relative to our respective positionalities. If we fail to seek these educational opportunities continually, how can we transform institutional culture without being complicit in manufacturing or reproducing the problems we say we wish to eradicate? Indeed, can we truly expect our efforts in DEI work to proffer anything short of what Damon A Williams and Katrina C. Wade-Golden refer to as "window-dressing diversity."[5]

If there is one challenge above others worth discussing for the benefit of new administrative leaders, it would be that of addressing and dealing forthrightly with interpersonal conflict. Addressing these dynamics can prove challenging, particularly when engaging faculty colleagues who have difficulty following rules and regulations or resent managerial authority whether or not one's leadership style is democratic in practice. For difficult faculty who revel in the degrees of autonomous privilege tenure affords, it may be necessary to hold them accountable through documented efforts and in consultation with a human resources representative. I offer these recommendations mindful of a faculty colleague who admits to having pursued life in academia from a desire of not wanting to have to work for someone. I have known other faculty-colleagues to subscribe to this same outlook. Additionally, and writing from my experiences in the military and in private industry, I do not think it hyperbole to state that new administrative leaders may find themselves astonished to know the types of unprofessional behaviors, bullying impulses, and poor decisions practiced by individual faculty colleagues.

All are to be managed appropriately and timely, and with a steadied resolve whereby one focuses on engaging colleagues fairly and dispassionately toward judiciously addressing the matter at hand. It is not a contradiction to offer that one can manage these types of conflict resolutely and dispassionately without dehumanizing those whose errors necessitate swift and appropriate response or action. Nor do I subscribe to managing such conflicts in a manner where one is subjugated to being bullied. I recommend leading from a posture that signals to all parties you and they are to be respected. Should a party conduct themselves unprofessionally, remain professional, honor your self-respect, and proceed through the agenda if it is possible to do so. If suspending the meeting and rescheduling proves an expedient option, it may be wise to do so, using the interim to seek additional guidance from one's human resource manager as may be necessary. It may even be necessary to establish and seek agreement from all parties at the outset of the meeting on the communication norms all will hold themselves accountable to when interacting with one another. Conflict avoidance is not an option. We must do the work we are entrusted to do without being unseemly or abused by others in the process.

When it comes to making tough, unpopular, and unfavorable decisions, do so and own them. No leader can or should expect to please everyone all the time. Following through processes of tough and challenging decision-making sometimes means leaders have to stand and bear the pain of being misunderstood, knowing that their resolve of holding fast to their convictions is not only right but in the best interest of the institution more importantly. In the event a given decision proves wrong or less than ineffectual, we should feel equally empowered to admit we were wrong. No administrative leader is perfect. Our mistakes do not define us. What matters most, I think, is how we handle and learn from them. Here, displays of leadership transparency, humility, and openness with constituent colleagues can go a very long way toward solidifying strong collaborative bonds with our colleagues. Our leadership benefits when our colleagues know they can trust us to be human and less than perfect before them.

As an African American leader within higher education, I cannot conclude without expressing the need for all administrative leaders to understand the difference that difference makes for professionals serving in billets of leadership from diverse and underrepresented backgrounds. Leading while black and/or Othered across axes of numerous and intersecting identity contingencies is a phenomenon that deserves the kind of scholarship devoted to chronicling the experiences of People of Color (POC) faculty in anthologies like *Race in the College Classroom*, and *Presumed Incompetence*. However well-meaning and good-intentioned colleagues and constituents throughout higher education might be, it is untenable and unprofessional to presume that race, class, gender, sexuality, neurodiversity, and a range of other prejudicial biases do not circulate the rooms people like me occupy when doing the work of administrative leadership at Predominantly White Institutions (PWIs). Macro and microaggressions, and even greater breaches to what Orlando Taylor, in another context, has identified as "anti-anyisms," circulate and reverberate throughout the professional spaces of academia. Whether overtly or covertly, these antagonisms prove especially pernicious because they may be difficult to name or challenging to raise to perpetrators whose tears, dismissals, and/or attitudinal responses create an exacerbating layer of conflict to an already dispiriting matter.

Conversations with other administrative leaders of color assure me that I am not alone in having these experiences. In the course of doing the work we were hired to do, we, at times, find ourselves challenged, disrespected, overlooked and misrepresented by colleagues both laterally and vertically. Because the leadership roles we now hold traditionally have been held and occupied by white men and with some increasing popularity, white women, cultural differences, ways of seeing, and ways of knowing sometimes contribute to the unintentional undermining of administrative leaders from underrepresented backgrounds. Senior administrative leaders who are well educated about the (in)visible workings of these biases and the impact they routinely have on direct reports from underrepresented backgrounds can prove most supportive when they, too, are attuned to the various social routes these dynamics might travel both laterally and vertically throughout institutions.

Conclusion: Finishing to Start Again

This essay is my effort to address many of the things I could not have known prior to transitioning from the faculty ranks and assuming the role of associate dean for academic affairs in my college. Since I started this essay, I have joined the faculty at Texas Christian University in my new role of dean for the School of Interdisciplinary Studies. I am beginning a new chapter, in which I continue to lead from my faculty perspective. I am proud of my varied experiences and accomplishments and am humbled further by the opportunity to serve students, staff, faculty-colleagues, and external publics in ways I never could within the enclosed spaces of English literature classrooms or on the printed pages of my published scholarship. I will not dare say that there is any one and ideal way to lead, serve, and support one's academic community in the capacity of an administrative leader. I do know that lessons learned along my nontraditional path continue to serve me well as I seek to advance as a faculty-colleague's most trusted academic leader, and that the work we all do on any given day in academia contributes to making the U.S. a more perfect union and the global society infinitely better than that which we individually inherited on the day we were born.

Notes

[1] I wish to acknowledge three organic intellectuals in my family whose wisdom informs key aspects of my leadership *ethos*: Anna Mixon Dicks, Shirley A. Bess, and Bernard Dicks.
[2] James M. Kouzes and Barry Z. Posner, *The Leadership Challenge* (Hoboken: John Wiley and Sons, 2017), 28.

[3] Nancy L. Zimpher, "Working the System: Cultivating Personnel Partnerships to Optimize University Systems," in *Leading Colleges and Universities: Lessons from Higher Education Leaders*, Eds. Stephen Joel Trachtenberg, Gerald B. Kauvar, and E. Gordon Gee (Baltimore: Johns Hopkins University Press, 2018), 236.

[4] I borrow this portmanteau from Manya Whitaker and Tina Valtierra, who coin the term in their collection, *Schooling Multicultural Teachers: A Guide for Professional Development and Program Assessment* (Bingley, UK: Emerald Publishing, 2019). Whitaker and Valtierra combine the words "thrive" and "survival" to express levels of success that exceed merely surviving given circumstances.

[5] Damon A. Williams and Katrina C. Wade-Golden, *The Chief Diversity Officer* (Sterling, VA: Stylus Publishing, 2013), 8.

Thirteen

From Here to Career:
A Circuitous Path toward Building
Undergraduate Career Services

Julie Candler Hayes

University of Massachusetts Amherst

Abstract

The essay describes the steps, planned and unplanned, in the development of career services for students in the arts and humanities at a public research university. What began as a modest one-credit "career prep" course has evolved over time into a well-staffed set of programs that demonstrates the interconnections among student services, college communications, development, and academic leadership; and has helped change the conversation about the humanities and careers at our institution.

Keywords: arts and humanities, career center, chair, communication skills, dean, enduring skills, French, Here 2 Career, job market, leadership, liberal arts, personnel, University of Massachusetts, Amherst

***

This essay has taken a circuitous path. It was initially planned as a practical how-to piece on setting up a career services center for arts and humanities students, then a more contemplative piece on lessons learned during the ten years of my deanship at the University of Massachusetts Amherst. In the end, my reflections on a decade in the dean's office led me back to the original idea: although our college accomplished many good things over the years, the career center is certainly one of the projects in which I take the most pride and whose effects will be most felt in the years to come. It is a work in progress, and like much of our work, whether teaching, scholarship, or service, it is evolving to meet the needs of the present. The many people who shaped its trajectory taught me a great deal about our institution and about the opportunities and limits of my role as dean.

I was an accidental dean in 2010. I was in my second term as a department chair when my dean was whisked away into the provost's office and I was asked to serve as interim dean of the College of Humanities and Fine Arts (HFA). I accepted the provost's request to serve with the assumption that I'd deepen my understanding of the institution and return to my department a more effective chair. A year later, I ended up applying for the deanship, something that wouldn't have occurred to me without the interim experience. My predecessor had recently added a student success coordinator position to our undergraduate advising center. Bright and entrepreneurial, she launched a number of programs, among them a one-credit, half-semester course on basic elements of the job search, such as resume writing, interviewing, etc. It was a modest effort, but at its heart was a powerful idea: that arts and humanities students possess important transferrable skills, that they can learn to articulate those skills and describe the relevance of their studies as they pursue their careers.

It seems painfully obvious to say that now, but it was novel for us then. As a French literature professor at a liberal arts college and later at UMass, for decades I'd taken as an article of faith that liberal arts students could take up any career path, but I had no specific knowledge to help them do that—I left that work to "career services." Upon arriving in the dean's office, I found that most of my colleagues felt the same way. Early on, when I asked our student success coordinator to present her career prep syllabus to the HFA Chairs' Council, one chair snorted, "We are not a job training center!"

The pathway that leads from that dispiriting moment to the present was not only filled with turns, but was also double: building an institutional framework on the one hand, while persuading many of the chairs and colleagues both that this was a worthwhile endeavor and that they should integrate its principles into their formal and informal advising practices, on the other.

I do not mean to imply that my colleagues were indifferent to their students or their fates after graduation; they are extraordinarily committed teachers and mentors, highly successful scholars and artists, and active citizens of the university and their professions. But they assumed, first, that they would always have robust enrollments and students eager to major in their departments, and second, that those students would manage well on the job market without any special effort from us. The second assumption may have been true for many years, but the job market was changing. The first assumption had been bolstered by the fact that our enrollments were strong and even growing in the first years after the 2008 recession: we told ourselves that we were a special place and that the "crisis in the humanities" was happening somewhere else. That optimistic picture began to fade after 2012, when students who with their families had heard the negative drum-beat about humanities and the job market for most of their teenage years began to arrive on campus and head straight for the professional schools and STEM majors.

Context. As its name indicates, the College of Humanities and Fine Arts contains a highly variegated set of departments large and small, from the traditional humanities fields and linguistics to the visual and performing arts and architecture, as well as several interdisciplinary departments. The arts disciplines and architecture regard themselves as (pre-)professional degree programs, but students throughout the college benefit from thinking of their future career trajectories in a broad context.

Let me begin with a simple narrative description of how our career services developed. The initial one-credit course provided a high-touch, deeply individualized experience that was much appreciated by a small number of students—twelve or fifteen in a section. From the outset, my question was how to scale it up to meet the needs of our college's 2400 majors. The two largest departments, English and History, offered their own career prep courses, but relatively few students were taking advantage of them; Women, Gender, Sexuality Studies offered its majors a well-established network of internship providers throughout the region.

The advising team and I discussed the possibility of converting the one-credit course to a set of online modules; ultimately, we settled on a series of linked workshops open to all students. Personnel turnover prevented the project from launching until the spring semester of 2015. Facilitated by the student success coordinator, the workshops offered a hands-on, discussion-oriented approach to different aspects of the job search and often included encounters with one or more alums whose careers exemplified the kind of versatility that we hoped would inspire students and give them confidence: from a comparative literature major to personal wealth management, for example; from philosophy to the gourmet food business, or from art history to finance and arbitrage. We gave the series a new name, "Here 2 Career," and rolled it out with posters and mailings. "Here 2 Career," or H2C became the college's brand for career prep programming, with the linked workshops in the spring; one-off events in the fall. The workshops attracted a fair number of students, but tended to level off at approximately thirty per session.

In a separate development, a decision at the university level to dissolve central Career Services in 2016 provided us with the opportunity to hire our long-time liaison, bringing her full-time into the college. (She had previously been the career services advisor to several colleges.) Caroline Gould brought with her years of experience, a deep knowledge of our college and ability to connect with our students, and excellent communication skills. Soon thereafter came the move of the renamed Advising & Career Center into renovated and expanded spaces adjacent to a large atrium popular with students, greatly enhancing its visibility. Caroline brought a wealth of ideas for reaching out to students: in addition to mailings and posters and her regular walk-in advising sessions, she created a career website, created sandwich boards linking HFA departments to the range of alumni professional trajectories, offered pop-up career advising in dormitories and other spaces around campus, made the rounds of departments to meet with faculty, visit classes, and consult on the development of department-based career courses and programming. Her energetic five-minute pep talks on career prep activities have become a fixture at our summer new student orientation sessions. In 2018 we expanded the operation by hiring an internship coordinator, supervised by Caroline, who maintains "functional" (dotted-line) supervision of the student success coordinator (who reports to the advising side).

Meanwhile, other moving parts were in play. As mentioned earlier, we've involved alumni in the workshops and other events, so the director of Development has an important role. Interactions with students are deeply appealing to alums. Through their conviction that they owe their professional success to perspectives and habits of mind nurtured through their engagement in the arts and humanities, alumni can be far more persuasive than those of us who never left the academy. During my first months as interim dean, I remember hearing the CEO (Chief Executive Officer) of a geothermal energy company describe why his undergraduate major in studio art had been a crucial part of his intellectual development: it was immensely heartening to hear him confirm something I had always believed, of course, and his story inspired me to bring his and other stories to students, through face-to-face meetings when possible, but also via written and video profiles.

Alumni engagement would be the subject of another essay. In the present context, I'll simply say that we progressed through trial and error. Few things are more disappointing than organizing an evening around a successful professional who is eager to share her story, and have only a handful of students appear. The Here 2 Career workshop series alleviated that problem to some degree, since it guaranteed that at least 25-30 students would be present. We also had successes with themed panels, sometimes tied to other events on campus: a group of HFA alums in technology careers, for example; or a panel of lawyers whose undergraduate majors ran the gamut from classics to art history and Afro-American Studies; or a group of alums in finance, who met with a joint class of literature and finance students.[1]

Often, the return to campus for an encounter with students was the first—and easiest—step toward engaging alumni who would go on to serve the college in other ways and to contribute financially. While many think first of scholarships when they are considering a gift, others have been attracted to our Internship Assistance Fund, which provides stipends to students engaged in meaningful, but unpaid summer internships in the arts and non-profit world.

If Development was one area in the dean's office that came to be an essential connection for career services, then Communications and Marketing was another. Even if students elected not to participate in career prep activities, we wanted them to be aware that opportunities existed throughout the college, both in our college career services office and at the departmental level. I liken the effect to that of living in a city or any vibrant cultural environment: one may not take advantage of everything, but the knowledge of the possibilities is part of the quality of life. Our goal was to normalize the presence of career guidance in our disciplines, as it is in the professional schools. We turned to multiple channels: newsletters, email and social media blasts, integrating career prep announcements with deadlines and information that the students relied on from the academic advising side. We asked the volunteer members of the Student Leadership Board to help spread the word about events.

I will not say that we have perfected this approach, but we have come a long way. One significant step was convening a meeting of the career services team from the dean's office with faculty and staff engaged in similar work at the departmental level, in order to foster awareness of each other's activities. The Theater department, for example, has long sponsored a regularly scheduled series of talks by theater professionals, often alumni, on career steps for budding actors, directors, and designers; for many years the Art department has run a course aimed at demystifying the New York art scene through meetings with artists, gallery owners, and critics. These have been deeply valuable encounters for students planning to make their way in the arts, but for students who study art, music, and theater, then choose to pursue a different path (such as financing geothermal projects), it's useful for them to know that less discipline-specific career preparedness opportunities are available as well.

The best-built career programs are pointless if no one knows about them, or if departments don't recommend them to students. While few faculty members today would voice the disdain evinced by my colleague a decade ago, I do not doubt that some continue to feel that utilitarian arguments framing the humanities as preparation for careers are misguided. At the same time, they deplore the shift in enrollments toward professional degrees and STEM fields widely viewed as more employable. Surely, however, it is not unreasonable for students and their families to show concern for their future after graduation. Well-publicized career-oriented events demonstrate that we recognize the importance of that concern, and that we are confident in our students' ability to venture into the world of work.

In his eloquent manifesto, *Why Choose the Liberal Arts?* Mark Roche argues that its three goals of liberal education—the formulation of a personal world view, the cultivation of the "practical virtues" in preparation for a career, and the discovery of a sense of purpose or vocation—are in no way mutually exclusive, but overlay and reinforce one another.[2] Roche goes on to suggest that "educators and career centers could do a better job of educating businesses about the capacities of liberal arts graduates."[3] I don't disagree, but I would argue that this is precisely what we should help our students do for themselves: to articulate the skills gained from their studies in ways that are of value to employers, such as research skills, problem-solving, teamwork and collaboration, ethical judgment, curiosity and ability to learn, appreciation of cultural and linguistic diversity. These "enduring skills" stand our students in good stead, particularly when paired with internship experiences or additional coursework that connects to a career field. Of course, we should all—administrators, faculty, concerned citizens—be making the case about the relevance of the humanities in as many contexts as we are able, inside and outside the academy. The "outside world" begins with students enrolled in introductory and general education classes: whatever discipline they eventually choose to major in, and whatever career they pursue, as citizens they will shape the society to come. By emphasizing both the intrinsic worth and the practical application of our intellectual work, we are defending the humanities from the ground up.

For many faculty members, the reluctance to engage with the issue of careers stems less from a rejection of an instrumentalizing approach to their discipline, than from a sense of a lack of expertise or ability to offer guidance. Our message has been: Not to worry! That is why we offer career services! Send the students here! The career center emails its calendar to undergraduate advisors and chairs; our goal has been to normalize references to the career center as an important resource for all students. In addition to that basic message, I've regularly raised the topic at meetings of the department chairs and at faculty meetings, inviting the Director of Career Services to talk about the work of the center, or a representative from a department with an active approach to career prep to give a presentation. It's worth noting that more departments than the two that I mentioned earlier now include some form of career guidance in their curriculum and programming. I continue to share materials that offer good grist for the mill: publications from the Georgetown Center on the Workplace, for example, the Humanities Indicators from the American Academy of Arts and Sciences, or the AAC&U (American Association of Colleges & Universities)'s surveys of employers, in hopes of stimulating conversations and raising awareness among the faculty.[4]

Did all this proceed smoothly and according to plan? Certainly not. We proceeded by trial and error. We took advantage of a number of unplanned and unforeseen developments, such as the dissolution of central career services. Indeed, tact and diplomacy were needed when I brought a career counselor with decades of experience into the team where the student success coordinator, whose background had been in student affairs, was teaching the career prep course. The growth of career services within the Advising Center, especially once we added the Internship Coordinator, created space problems—when we had begun planning for the building renovations, no one expected the additional staff positions. There have also been moments of friction between the needs of the career services group, who often need to seize and publicize opportunities on short notice, and the communications area, which needs to oversee materials for content and adherence to brand. Or the frustration of both Development and Career Services when they learn that a department just invited an alum to meet with students, but didn't let us know or advertise it outside the department.

None of these issues constitute an insuperable problem. In retrospect, I can see that what initially appeared to be a particular project, launching a course/workshop on job-hunting skills, would ultimately draw on multiple areas in college operations, and on all my leadership, personnel management, and communications skills. As we worked together on the circuitous path towards "Here 2 Career," I was discovering, in a roundabout fashion, one of the most important through-lines of my own career.

H2C remains a work in progress. 2019 saw a major development, when we decided to offer the workshop series in the fall semester and over seventy students tried to register. Unfortunately, it was scheduled in a room that could only hold thirty, and by the time a new room was located, the long waiting list had largely melted away. We were elated by the demand, but it pointed to the need for a new approach. Instead of the series of linked workshops, we decided that it was time to create a full-semester, credit-bearing course, offered either in multiple sections or in a team-based learning format, or combination of the two. The opportunity arose to hire an instructor with exceptional pedagogical skills and experience with both career prep and alumni relations, to redesign the course and offer it in Fall 2020. Meanwhile, in the spring of 2020, the disruption wrought by the pandemic forced career services to go online, like everything else. As faculty were learning over the course of spring break to teach remotely, the advisors and career counselors did the same. In addition to the wealth of information on majors and career tracks on the Careers & Internships webpage, they added a new link to "Remote and Virtual Opportunities," which has become one of the most-consulted pages in the entire college.[5] The new and expanded H2C is ready to launch—remotely, for now, but with no enrollment cap—in Fall 2020.

Looking back, I am happy with what we have been able to accomplish. I am particularly happy that, after several years of declining enrollments, the numbers have been steadily rising since 2017. Even at an institution like UMass, with an ethos favorable to the arts and humanities and cognizant of the intellectual capital represented in our departments, it is clearly a relief to be able to point to positive enrollment trends. While there are undoubtedly many factors at play in this development—just as there were in our decline—I credit the growth and enhanced visibility of our career center for part of this success.

Not that students are running to major in Classics because of its career opportunities, but, rather, students who arrive at the university with a fascination with ancient languages and cultures, or who discover that passion in a general education course, will have the confidence that they will be able to tell their own story about why they embarked on this course of study, why it is valuable, and what it enables them to bring to the workplace.

Notes

[1] This was a course team-taught by faculty in Comparative Literature and Finance for students in both departments, intended to provide insights into the finance world for the literature students, and train the finance majors in techniques of textual analysis, applied to corporate documents and reports.

[2] Mark William Roche, *Why Choose the Liberal Arts?* (Notre Dame, IN: University of Notre Dame Press, 2010), especially Chapter 2, "Cultivating Intellectual and Practical Virtues," 51-99. Roche counters those who shun any utilitarian view of the liberal arts by offering a thoughtful discussion of the "intellectual virtues" that have demonstrable value in the active life, such as communication and writing skills, critical thinking, and global thinking.

[3] Roche, 96.

[4] See, for example, the reports and advocacy toolkits available from the Council of Colleges of Arts and Sciences https://www.ccas.net/i4a/pages/index.cfm?pageid=3975 ; the Association of American Colleges and Universities https://www.aacu.org/public-opinion-research; the American Academy of Arts and Sciences (in particular the "Humanities Indicators" project) https://www.amacad.org/topic/arts-humanities ; and the Georgetown University Center on Education and the Workforce https://cew.georgetown.edu.

[5] https://www.umass.edu/hfa/advising/careers

Fourteen

Side Jobs and Academic Service

Paula M. Krebs

Modern Language Association

Abstract

Some faculty members are really good at teaching. Some are best at research. But the ones who are good at both those things and always seem to find themselves adding other items to their plates—service projects, grants administration, chairing tenure committees—those are the folks who make the best academic administrators. If you always seem to have a side gig going, you may enjoy, and probably will be good at, being a dean.

Keywords: chair, curricular planning, editorship, English, deanship, equity, feminist literary criticism, first-generation, humility, Indiana University, labor practices, liberal education, literary analysis, newspaper editing, research, scholarship, service, students of color, teaching, working-class

***

I always had a side job.

That's probably the most significant factor in my move into campus administration and, eventually, into off-campus leadership. I was never totally secure in academia, never sure that the profession I'd stumbled into would be a comfortable home. So I always had an exit strategy, something I was working on that was not directly part of my job, but that was doing the kind of work I thought needed doing. Those side hustles, the work that was not the work, have been what has enabled me to construct the career I have. This career, neither a traditional academic career nor a traditional administrative career, is the career that fits me. I will tell you how I got here, and you can decide whether the route, or a similar one, would work for you.

As a first-generation college student, I fell in love with writing, research and literary analysis after I flunked out of my physics major. I had been a student journalist in high school, and I turned that work into paid work for my local newspaper when I was in college, so I knew I had the tools to make a living. Taking classes I loved seemed like the thing to do, since I knew I'd have the experience to get a job at a newspaper after I graduated. But I was pretty good in those literature classes, and one day a teacher suggested I think about graduate school. Keep doing research and writing essays about this stuff I loved? Yes, please!

During my senior year, when reading an article in an issue of *Victorian Studies*, I saw an ad for an editorial assistant for the journal, which was produced at Indiana University (IU). I could do that, I figured, since I was already a working journalist (alright, a sportswriter—but how hard could the transition be?). The editorial assistant, I saw, got free tuition at Indiana plus a stipend. It seemed like a good deal. So I applied to the IU PhD program in English and for the job.

The next thing I knew, I had heard from the department that 1) new graduate students were not eligible for the editorial assistantship but 2) the department had put me up for a fellowship instead, and I had gotten it. Even better! Free money for a year, followed by four years of a teaching assistantship.

Sometime during my first year in graduate school, I learned that a PhD in English was meant to lead to a particular career outcome—a job as a faculty member. It may seem odd to you, but as a first-gen college student, I had never thought to ask why someone would get a PhD. It just seemed like a fun and challenging thing to do after college and before whatever came next. Even though I was first-gen, I'd never thought of college as preparing one for a particular job, and it hadn't occurred to me that graduate school did that either. And, even though today much public discourse focuses on the bachelor's degree as workforce preparation, a liberal arts degree, now, as then, prepares one to learn a multitude of careers, not one particular job.

But just because becoming a faculty member was the desired outcome of my PhD program didn't mean that I committed myself to a single-minded pursuit of it. All through graduate school I continued to work as a journalist, at the town's daily paper and then at a magazine. I took on editing jobs on the side. I needed to know that I could still make a living if this professor thing didn't work out. Once, when I arrived late at a party at a faculty member's house, the host asked what I'd been doing. I explained that I was late because I'd just gotten off my shift at the newspaper. He was astonished. Not judgmental, but perplexed: he said to me "I could never do anything other than be a professor." "How sad," I remember thinking.

And I think that if you want to make a career in which you can do something beyond scholarship and teaching, it's important to do things beyond scholarship and teaching—while you are a faculty member. The best administrators are people who can think about more than one thing at a time—more than one thing, and more than one kind of thing. Teaching, scholarship, and developing programming. Teaching, labor practices, and curricular planning. Research, fundraising, and assessment. **Lesson one: You have to be able to think of yourself as someone who can do many things well, and you can't be afraid to do them all at once.**

Back to my story: When I was in graduate school, my friends and I were in a feminist literary criticism reading group, and we noticed how none of the stuff we were reading addressed the half of our professional lives that was not research: our teaching. So we decided to start a publication about feminist pedagogy. I wrote and edited for the local daily newspaper, so I was able to get the copy typeset, and I had the copy-editing skills we needed. Editing that publication got me my first academic job, because I could train students as editorial assistants, and that fit well with the values of this liberal arts institution. It never occurred to me that publishing a pedagogy magazine would get me a job, but it made me attractive to at least one institution, and that was all I needed. I edited that publication, working happily with talented undergraduate editorial assistants and the rest of the magazine's founders, for the first few years of my faculty job, and after I passed on the editorship, it continued to pay dividends.

Now it's important to stop here and acknowledge some salient facts. One, I am a white woman. That gave me all kinds of advantages I didn't even think about as I pursued these side hustles. It's all well and good to tell graduate students to pursue side interests while they are completing their degrees, but the fact is that graduate students of color face a range of constraints that mean that when they pursue interests beside the strictly academic, they may be seen by white faculty members as less serious, not more ambitious. My own white working-class background prompted me to work side jobs and keep my options open in graduate school, but I was able to do that because there was no obvious outward indicator of my class, no signal to faculty members that I was a student who might not bring the same cultural capital to the program or who was not an easy "fit" in the department.

I was asked to apply for the editorship of a magazine for a national faculty organization, and my experience in journalism got me that gig. The editorship allowed me to flex those journalism muscles and also to have some influence on a national stage. I met lots of folks and commissioned good articles and got to help set an agenda for a national conversation about pedagogy, academic freedom, and campus labor practices. I was able to try to make some change nationally at the same time as I was working on campus, as a department chair, trying to do some good work locally.

The next opportunity that came up was another national one: as department chair, I had become involved in the professional development arm of the Modern Language Association, my disciplinary association. The professional development work in the MLA is largely done through MLA Academic Program Services (the Association of Departments of English and the Association of Departments of Foreign Language), and I took full advantage of what those more experienced department chairs had to teach me at their annual summer seminars. When I was elected to the committee that did the planning itself, I served gladly, learning much from my fellow chairs all over the US and Canada. Eventually I was appointed to work on an ad hoc committee on a topic I cared about, and that committee came to the conclusion that what we needed to do was apply for a grant to run an institute. No one else in the group wanted to do it, so I said I would.

Getting that grant and running the subsequent project for seven years, on a course release from my institution, gave me administrative experience that proved more valuable than anything I accumulated as a chair. Among other things, it enabled me to make a tiny dent in a national problem (the problem of the underrepresentation of students of color in PhD programs in English), and it taught me how to work with a foundation, how to work with scholars who knew much more than I did about the students I was trying to serve, and how to make changes during a program to make it more successful. Rather than trying to run the program myself, I assembled a powerhouse steering committee of scholars from all over the country who were committed to the idea of the program and willing to invest their time in helping design it. My least successful projects came when I had ideas myself and tried to convince people to support them; my most successful ones were projects that drew on the ideas of people who were more expert than I. **Lesson two: Combine your ambition to get something done with humility—because there's always someone who knows a lot more about it than you do.**

My experience of administration has shown me how important it is to realize that you cannot do much of anything on your own. Successful academic administration comes from recognizing who is better situated than you are to get something done and then leveraging their interest and strengths to make something happen. This can only happen when your interests align with those of the folks you want to work with—asking someone to put in extra work for a project just because you think it's important is a recipe for disaster, whether the person you're asking is below you or above you in the higher ed hierarchy.

When I moved into a deanship after being a department chair, I learned just how important it is to gather the right people into your work. That applies on campus and off campus, and it is especially relevant now, when gathering is possible through online platforms in ways it never was before. You can have all the great ideas in the world, but unless you have established relationships with people who share your ideals and are willing to work with you, you will be unable to move any project forward. In fact, you might want to think about your organizing abilities before you decide you want to move into administration. That is, if you are good at getting the work done, in your department or on your campus or in your home, you might be thinking, "I'm good at this—maybe I should be a dean." If you can keep things moving along smoothly, people are probably very grateful to you (whether they say it or not).

But here's what you need to ask yourself if you are considering moving into administration: when's the last time I fixed something that was broken? A bad process in your department, a bottleneck at your institution, a fundraising muddle in your PTA (Parent Teacher Association) or other community group? Getting the work done is not enough—or it shouldn't be. Although you will face many obstacles as an administrator, and there will be lots of things you can't fix, the only reason to apply for a deanship is that you want to make things better and think you can.

What I learned as a graduate student, as a faculty member who organized projects outside my department and my institution, and as a dean was that I could get people together to make things happen. That's what produces change in higher education—the faith that you can make something happen and the ability to convince other people to work with you to do it. If you've noticed a need, other people have noticed it, too, and they can help you fix it. My most successful projects as a dean involved putting people in a room together to brainstorm solutions to problems we all recognized. **Lesson three: Fixing things is more important than keeping things going.**

When I moved from a senior faculty position at a good liberal arts college to a deanship at a regional public university, there were some raised eyebrows at my college. People wondered, and in some cases came right out and asked, why on earth would one take a step down the prestige ladder? I wanted to make change at an institution whose students were more like the student I had been: working class, first-generation college. I wanted to learn more about public higher education and how it worked, and I wanted to see what kind of difference I could make. It was not easy to move sectors. There was a lot of distrust of the private-college faculty member who had arrived as the new dean at my university. But I had proved my bona fides by doing an American Council of Education ACE Fellowship the year before at the state flagship university, which I had chosen so I could learn about how state higher education functioned in terms of both finance and policy.

When I interviewed for my deanship, someone asked me how long I'd stay in the job. That's a trap, of course, but I answered as honestly as I could, "As long as I'm still learning." And I meant it. I knew it would take me a while to learn the ins and outs of a regional public university and to learn what kinds of things worked well and what could use some fixing. Then it took some time to learn what kind of fixing worked and what kind didn't. After five years, I felt that I had accumulated a good understanding of public higher education to go with my two decades of experience in a small liberal arts environment, and it was time for a new challenge.

The next logical step was a provost or president position, and I interviewed for a fair few. But I knew my heart wasn't in it. It seemed as if I were just looking for the next thing, at a campus whose mission I could get behind. And that's fine; that's good. But it wasn't where I needed to be. I knew that the service I wanted to do (and, of course, administrative work is service work) was service at a national level. I applied for a couple of jobs that stretched me, jobs at which I'd have a lot to learn but where I could ultimately, it seemed to me, make a difference. Nothing quite worked until I started thinking about the job I currently hold, with a disciplinary society.

This kind of position, at a professional association, would not appeal to everyone in higher education—it's not campus-based, it involves supervising a range of different activities, including membership functions, book publication, a research database, a convention and member events, and professional development offerings. But my interest in it grew from my interest in and commitment to the association throughout my career. I had given my time to committees and served on the board of this association, so I knew what it did and had ideas about what it could do. I went into the application, and the job, with my eyes wide open.

For me, this position is the happy ending of a career that was built on extras. After decades of extra jobs and projects, most of which added national work to local jobs, I ended up getting to do the national work as the local job. I advocate for the humanities and for higher education, I help people to gather, in person and remotely, to share their research and pedagogy. I get to work with humanities leaders from all over the country who have better ideas than I do and who are willing to let me poach them. And I get to provide services for a membership that is dedicated to the same things as I am: liberal education, equity in employment and teaching, student success, humanities research, access to information, and much more. In the middle of a global pandemic, it feels good to be dedicated to service, to helping members with teaching resources and emergency grants, to converting our convention to a virtual one so people can still present their research and workshops and find ways to connect with each other.

This association executive position involves all the things I used to do on the side: applying for grants, writing articles, organizing groups of experts to solve problems. And I get to do it all in service to language and literature education, which is what got me into graduate school in the first place. I know I have benefited from luck and privilege on this journey, and this position is a good one in which to pave the way for folks without access to that privilege. But whether you choose to pursue work in a disciplinary association or not, staying active in yours offers lots of good opportunities for service and for administrative experience. Committee work, board work, and project work can all add to your skills at the same time as it supports the field you love. You meet lots of folks who care about what you care about, and you can work with people on projects that make a difference to the discipline.

I guess that's the final lesson, really. If what you want to do is make a difference outside the classroom, administrative work is a good way to go. There's nothing like helping students transform their lives, certainly—teaching is rewarding as few other occupations can be. But for me, I knew there were lots of people who could teach well and could do my job as well as I could. What I wasn't convinced of was that there were lots of people who could organize projects, bring people together to make change, and help faculty members find the ways to do their jobs even better. I thought I could help the profession, the faculty, the students, and the humanities by doing a different kind of administration. You'll find the right path for you, if you're in it for the right reasons. So I leave you with this: **Lesson Four: Administration is service; choose whom you want to serve, and you'll always feel good about the work you're doing.**

Contributors

Frederick J. Antczak is Professor of English and the founding Dean of the College of Liberal Arts and Sciences at Grand Valley State. He has held positions at the University of California-Berkeley, the University of Virginia, and the University of Iowa. He has served as President and then as Executive Director of the Rhetoric Society of America.

Kate Conley is Professor of French & Francophone Studies and Chancellor Professor of Modern Languages and Literatures at William & Mary, where she formerly served as Dean of the Faculty of Arts & Sciences. She has also served as Associate Dean for Arts and Humanities and Chair of French and Italian at Dartmouth College. Her scholarship focuses on surrealism.

Valerio Ferme is Provost at the University of Cincinnati, where he has also served as Dean of the College of Arts and Sciences. He has previously served as Dean of the College of Arts and Letters at the University of Northern Arizona, and as Divisional Dean of Arts and Humanities and Chair of the Department of French and Italian and at the University of Colorado-Boulder.

Sheryl I. Fontaine is Dean of the College of Humanities and Social Sciences and Professor of English at California State, Fullerton. She teaches Composition and Rhetoric and has served as Associate Dean of Administration; Chair of the Department of English, Comparative Literature, and Linguistics; Writing Center Coordinator, and Director of the University Learning Center.

Claire Oberon Garcia is Dean of the Faculty, Acting Provost, and Professor English at Colorado College. She has previously served as Department Chair and Director of the Race, Ethnicity and Migration Studies Program. Her scholarship focuses on Black Women Writers in Twentieth Century Paris and critical perspectives on white-authored narratives of Black life.

Bonnie Gunzenhauser is Dean of the College of Arts and Sciences at John Carroll University. She previously served as Dean of the College of Arts and Sciences at Roosevelt University in Chicago. Her scholarship focuses on the literature and culture of England's long eighteenth century and the public humanities.

Emily A. Haddad is Dean of the College of Liberal Arts and Sciences at the University of Maine. She previously served as Associate Dean for Academics in the College of Arts and Sciences at University of South Dakota, where she also served as Chair of the English Department. Her background is in Comparative Literature.

Timothy D. Hall is Dean of Howard College of Arts and Sciences at Samford University. He previously served as Associate Dean at the College of Humanities and Social and Behavioral Sciences at Central Michigan University, where he also served as Chair of the Department of History. His background is in colonial American and Atlantic World history.

Julie Candler Hayes is Professor of French at the University of Massachusetts Amherst, where she has served as Dean of the College of Humanities and Fine Arts, after serving as Chair of Literatures, Cultures, and Cultures. She previously served as department chair at the University of Richmond. She is a past president of the American Society for Eighteenth-Century Studies.

Paula M. Krebs is Executive Director for the Modern Language Association, the largest scholarly organization in organization in the humanities. She previously served as Dean of the College of Humanities and Social Sciences at Bridgewater State University, after serving as Chair of the English department at Wheaton College.

Michelle A. Massé is McElveen Professor of English and Affiliate of Women's and Gender Studies at Louisiana State University, where she has previously served as Dean of the Graduate School, Interim Vice Provost for Graduate Studies, Acting Associate Dean of the College of Humanities and Social Sciences, and Founding Director of Women's and Gender Studies.

Shaily Menon is Dean of the College of Arts and Sciences at the University of New Haven. She previously served as Dean of the College of Arts and Sciences for four years at Saint Joseph's University, and as Associate Dean in the College of Liberal Arts and Sciences at Grand Valley State University. Her background is in conservation biology and biodiversity informatics.

Karen Petersen is Dean of the Kendall College of Arts & Sciences and Professor of Political Science at the University of Tulsa. She previously served as Dean of the College of Liberal Arts at Middle Tennessee State University.

Reginald A. Wilburn is Dean for the School of Interdisciplinary Studies at Texas Christian University. He previously served as Associate Dean for Academic Affairs in the College of Liberal Arts at the University of New Hampshire, where he was also Associate Professor of English. His background is in Milton, African American literature, and intertextuality studies.

Index

P

pandemic, xi, xii, xiii, 10, 11, 12,
23, 43, 45, 47, 55, 56, 57, 61, 62,
67, 71, 73, 107, 113, 114, 115,
122, 123, 143, 150; Pandemic
Response Team, 35, 44; pre-
pandemic, 122, 123, see also,
team, crisis response team
path of self discovery, 47, 48;
pilgrim's, 3, 4
People of Color (POC), 7, 61; see
also, Black, Indigenous People
of Color (BIPOC)
personnel, 6, 31, 41, 52, 57, 84, 85,
90, 97, 99, 97, 99, 136, 137, 139,
143
Petersen, Karen, xiii, 97
Pfaff, Thomas J., 95
philosophy, 68
Pink, Daniel, 123
plague, 56; see also, pandemic
The Plague, see Camus
plot, 25, 26, 29, 30, 31, 32
point-of-view, 25, 26, 39
political science, 78; political
scientist, 99
politics, 70, 97, 98
Posner, Barry Z., 26, 135
Predominantly White Institutions
(PWI)
president, 8, 12, 22,23, 26, 42, 45,
52, 53, 54, 55, 56, 62, 63, 64, 65,
69, 82, 85, 86, 92, 100, 123, 128,
129, 130, 150
pre-tenure faculty, 35, 39, 67, 85 ;
junior faculty, 15, 17, 21, 22, 27,
37, 42, 68, 69, 98; see also, early
career faculty, 3, 4
private institutions, xi, 3, 4, 20, 71;
college, 149; university, 20, 124

professional development, 6, 9, 35,
37, 84, 89, 91, 92, 93, 99, 102,
136, 147, 150
Project on the Rhetoric of Inquiry
(POROI), see rhetoric
promotion, 8, 15, 16, 17, 18, 21, 36,
37, 38, 39, 49, 54, 69, 81, 84, 85,
112, 125; promoted 16, 68, 85,
119
provost, 16, 23, 26, 29, 32, 42, 43,
45, 47, 48, 52, 55, 56, 57, 62, 69,
80, 81, 82, 85, 86, 87, 89, 99, 100,
103, 119, 121,123, 138, 150
public humanities, 47, 50
public institutions, xi, 3, 4, 20, 51,
124; higher education, 71, 115,
124; minority-serving, 107;
university, 20, 40, 76, 79, 101,
107, 149
public relations (PR), 83

Q

Quinn, Arthur, 77

R

Race, Ethnicity, and Migration
Program, see Ethnic Studies
*Race in the College Classroom and
Presumed Incompetence,* 134
racism, 62, 64, 66, 70, 71; racial,
6,16, 63, 70, 112; racial strife,
62, 72; racist, 61, 62, 64, 66; see
also, antiracism
rank, 8, 12, 15, 16, 18, 21, 32, 68,
79, 87
Reiksuniversiteit Groningen, 35,
36
relationship, 25, 49, 50, 54, 66, 68,
72, 112, 120; relationships, 12,
26, 35, 37, 38, 41, 50, 53, 54, 69,

CPSIA information can be obtained
at www.ICGtesting.com
Printed in the USA
BVHW031954181022
649650BV00012B/87/J

9 781648 891953